Profiles in Journalistic Courage

Profiles in Journalistic Courage

editors
Robert Giles
Robert W. Snyder
Lisa DeLisle

Routledge
Taylor & Francis Group

LONDON AND NEW YORK

Originally published in the *Media Studies Journal*, Spring/Summer 2000.

Published 2001 by Transaction Publishers

Published 2017 by Routledge
2 Park Square, Milton Park, Abingdon, Oxon OX14 4RN
711 Third Avenue, New York, NY 10017, USA

Routledge is an imprint of the Taylor & Francis Group, an informa business

Library of Congress Catalog Number: 00-066962

Library of Congress Cataloging-in-Publication Data

Profiles in journalistic courage / Robert Giles, Robert W. Snyder, Lisa DeLisle,
editors.
    p. cm.
  Originally published in the Media studies journal, Spring/Summer 2000.
  Includes bibliographical references and index.
  ISBN 0-7658-0796-3 (pbk. : alk. paper)
    1. Journalists-- Biography. 2. Journalism--Political aspects. I. Giles,
Robert H., 1933– II. Snyder, Robert W., 1955– III. DeLisle, Lisa. IV. Media
studies journal.

PN4820.P76 2001
070.92'2—dc21   00-066962

ISBN 13: 978-0-7658-0796-0 (pbk)

Contents

Preface   xi

Part 1: Yesterday

1. The Zenger Trial   3
    David Copeland

A professor of mass communication examines a venerable story and finds, in light of scholarship, a challenging conclusion: "The trial of John Peter Zenger had little to do with freedom of the press in colonial America. It had much to do with political control and partisanship in New York."

2. David Ruggles   11
    Graham Russell Hodges

"David Ruggles, an African-American printer in New York City during the 1830s, was the prototype for black activist journalists of his time," writes a historian. "His career epitomized the fusion of professionalism and activism, so characteristic of later black journalists, that would propel him to the center of racial conflict."

3. Francisco P. Ramírez   19
    Félix Gutiérrez

"Less than a decade after Los Angeles residents had seen the border between the United States and Mexico redrawn to leave them inside the United States, Californios had become strangers in their own land," writes a media analyst. "They looked for guidance. Some found it in the words of Francisco P. Ramírez, teen-age editor of the first Spanish-language newspaper of Los Angeles, *El Clamor Público* (The Public Outcry)."

4. Ida B. Wells-Barnett   29
    Pamela Newkirk

"On May 4, 1884, more than 70 years before Rosa Parks fueled the civil rights movement by refusing to give up her seat on a bus to a white man, 22-year-old Ida B. Wells spurned a segregated train car to sit in the ladies' coach," writes a professor. "After writing about her legal battle in a religious newsweekly, Wells would for another four decades use journalism as a weapon against the virulent racial bigotry sweeping the South."

5. Robert Capa and the Spanish Civil War   37
    Richard Whelan

"From 1936 to 1954, Robert Capa photographed five wars and set the standard by which photojournalists are judged," his biographer writes. "Of all the conflicts he covered it was his first, the Spanish Civil War, that established his defining characteristics: passionate commitment, readiness to take sides, a willingness to share the hardships of the people he photographed and an ability to reconcile great ideals with sympathy and respect for individuals."

6. The Journalism of the French Resistance   45
    Pierre Albert

"The first publishers of underground sheets were journalists by chance," writes a French press historian. "Political party militants, labor unionists, academics, members of the professions, students, writers, clergymen, lawyers and army officers switched to journalism—and were surprised to discover how easy it was to express their indignation and enthusiasm in short columns, or to comment upon events that they heard about on the radio or in the regular papers."

7. This Female Crusading Scalawag   55
    Bernard L. Stein

An editor goes to Mississippi to research the life and legacy of Hazel

Brannon Smith, an editor who supported the civil rights movement: "Her nationwide fame has faded, her name is unfamiliar to a new generation of journalists, but her African-American readers in Holmes County remember her vividly to this day."

8. L. Alex Wilson   67
    Hank Klibanoff

An African-American reporter who once ran from white racists and vowed never to run again was assigned to cover the Little Rock, Arkansas, integration crisis. "The day would be as fateful for Wilson," an author writes, "as it was for the nine Little Rock students and for the nation."

Part 2: Today

9. Letizia Battaglia   79
    Alexander Stille

"Letizia Battaglia began to photograph the Sicilian Mafia in 1974, long before it was popular, chic, convenient or particularly safe to do so," writes an author and authority on Italian organized crime. "The powerful images she created gave faces and corporeal reality to and helped awaken public awareness of a phenomenon that was tragically ignored for decades to the detriment of Sicily and Italy as a whole."

10. Picturing Breast Cancer   89
    Betty Rollin

An author, journalist and breast cancer survivor interviews two women, Matuschka and Ned Asta, who survived breast cancer and showed their scars to the camera.

11. Great Courage, Small Places   99
    Eric Newton and Mary Ann Hogan

"The social geometry here is fundamental: smaller people, by definition, face bigger obstacles," argue two writers. "And so, in the end, a fitting epigraph to the great-courage, small-places pantheon might be: the less power you have, the more courage you need."

12. Glasnost Betrayed   107
    Emma Gray

In Russia, too many journalists have found ways to make their peace with corruption and intimidation, a journalist and activist writes. "They have been won over by the forces of fear, money and cynicism. The consequences of such behavior are dire for journalism itself and for the future of democracy in Russia."

13. Jeffrey Schmalz   115
    Richard J.Meislin

A *Times*man recalls how his colleague's struggle with AIDS changed *The New York Times*. "For many of his colleagues it was the first time they had worked side by side with—or even knew personally—someone fighting AIDS, and the scorecard of the battle was frequently evident in his personal appearance, or his presence or absence."

14. Native American Newspapers   121
    Mark N. Trahant

"Sometimes you have to publish stories that your bosses would prefer remain hidden away from view," writes a veteran of Native American newspapers. "You have to regularly ask yourself what becomes the first question of native journalism: do you work for your readers or for those who are elected to govern a tribal nation?"

15. Breaking Ranks in Northern Ireland   131
    Malachi O'Doherty

"One of the core ideas of working-class politics," a journalist from Belfast writes, "promoted by both Loyalist and Republican paramilitaries, is the need for community cohesion and solidarity around the cause. The paramilitary organizations on both sides have tried to monopolize the expression of the areas they occupy. Contradict them and you are not just a traitor to a political cause, you are a defector from your own root community."

16. Church and State   141
    Leo Bogart

"The head of an individually or family-owned media business may be more willing to take risks than the chief executive of a publicly held company worried about the reaction from Wall Street," notes a veteran media analyst. "But in today's corporate economy, editorial independence does not always jibe with the demands of the bottom line."

17. Courage Isn't Enough   151
    John Owen

"I realize that the willingness to go into dangerous places was not enough to guarantee my safety, the safety of anyone who worked with me or our ability to capture an important story and bring it home to our viewers," writes a former international television producer. "We all desperately needed the kind of training for 'hostile environments' that is now readily available in Britain for journalists who are about to be dispatched to their first conflict."

18. Freedom Neruda   159
    W. Joseph Campbell

"The case of Freedom Neruda," a professor and former African correspondent writes, "is in several respects emblematic of the quiet courage of journalists in French-speaking West Africa, a region where a surprisingly resilient—yet little recognized—ethos of independent journalism has emerged and taken hold since the early 1990s."

Review Essay: Different Faces of Courage

19. Who Has Guts?   169
    James Boylan

A veteran media analyst explores different kinds of journalistic bravery, including "the courage to resist legal and physical threats on one's native ground, the courage to risk danger to tell disquieting news to the world of the comfortable, the (corporate) courage to offer audiences what they do not necessarily want to hear, and the courage to become a dissident inside an organization."

For Further Reading   179

Index   183

Preface

IF HISTORY IS USUALLY WRITTEN about the winners, stories of courage are usually written about the famous. Yet some of the bravest actions of journalists are unknown—obscured by the passage of time, hidden by veils of anonymity or buried by systematic repression. The "Courage" issue of Media Studies Journal aims to correct this imbalance.

With a few exceptions, the stories that we tell are not the familiar tales that journalists recount when they want to establish the heroism of their craft—Ernie Pyle covering World War II, *The New York Times* publishing the Pentagon Papers, *The Washington Post* exposing Watergate. Instead, we found examples from, in the words of Richard Whelan on Robert Capa, "the edge of things." Our subjects are primarily journalists who worked on the margins of popularity, who blazed new but solitary paths or who left fleeting legacies. Their lives and their work are a reminder that tests of integrity usually occur far from the spotlight. Perhaps that is why brave journalists are reluctant to speak of themselves as such: they know that there are others, not lucky enough to gain fame, who are equally deserving of recognition.

Even if our subjects found notoriety in their own time, they were not always thanked for their bravery. Jealousy, political disagreements and differing conceptions of journalism have fueled criticism of some of the people that we cite here for courage. This reporter's principled stand is that reporter's grandstanding. Another reporter's courageous exclusive can be a publisher's nightmare.

To complicate the subject further, brave journalists, like others who put themselves at risk, do not always act for reasons that win popularity or acclaim. Actions with laudable consequences can be the result of egotism, stubbornness and ignorance, as well as selflessness, prudence and principle. Finally, it is worth recognizing that for all the emphasis that American journalism places on the virtues of detachment, some of the most admirable journalists brought to life in these pages—Ida B. Wells-Barnett, Robert Capa, Letizia Battaglia—entered journalism with a sense of commitment to a cause that they never abandoned. Capa, Wells-Barnett and Battaglia also stand out for the recognition they achieved in their own lifetimes.

Few journalists can look forward to becoming famous heroes, but most can expect to have their fortitude tested in a lonely place. Let the lives examined in these essays be an example when that time comes.

THIS VOLUME SPANS the past and the present. In "Yesterday," David Copeland examines the tangled legacy of the trial of John Peter Zenger. Graham Russell Hodges unearths the story of David Ruggles, an African-American journalist and abolitionist in New York City during the 1830s. Félix Gutiérrez explores Francisco P. Ramírez's response to Yankee conquest in 19th-century California. Sarah L. Rasmusson interprets a photograph of women selling a suffragist newspaper. Pamela Newkirk recalls the life and work of Ida B. Wells-Barnett, journalist and anti-lynching activist.

Robert W. Snyder interprets a Frank Hurley photograph of the Shackleton Expedition. Richard Whelan presents Robert Capa's vision of the Spanish Civil War. Pierre Albert explains the journalism of the French Resistance. Bernard L. Stein brings to light the story of Hazel Brannon Smith, an editor who supported the civil rights movement. Hank Klibanoff explores the work and motivations of L. Alex Wilson, a civil rights reporter.

In "Today," Alexander Stille chronicles the work of Letizia Battaglia, the anti-Mafia photographer from Palermo, Sicily. Betty Rollin interviews two women who revealed the physical scars of their breast cancer surgery. Eric Newton and Mary Ann Hogan meditate on why the greatest journalistic courage is often found in the smallest places.

Examining the recent history of Russian journalism, Emma Gray shows why bravery has been the exception rather than the rule. In a photo taken during fighting in Chechnya, Jonathan Sanders explores the work of an American photographer who practiced the journalism of commitment. Richard J. Meislin shows how one journalist's reporting, along with his own public battle with AIDS, helped to change the lives of gay people at *The New York Times*. Mark N. Trahant looks at struggles for press freedom in Native American tribal journalism. From Northern Ireland, Malachi O'Doherty meditates on the causes, burdens and benefits of reporting that break with communal beliefs. Leo Bogart looks at the need to maintain a healthy and honorable relationship between business and editorial interests at media organizations. John Owen considers the kinds of training that are necessary to ensure the safety of international reporters in dangerous situations. Looking at struggles for press freedom in West Africa, W. Joseph Campbell finds heroism that is not widely reported in the American press.

Finally, in "Review Essay," James Boylan examines a history, an annual report, two memoirs and a feature film that offer varied perspectives on different aspects of the subject of courage in journalism: the courage to resist threats, the courage to tell people what they don't want to hear and the courage to become a dissident inside an organization.

—THE EDITORS

Part 1

YESTERDAY

1

The Zenger Trial

Partisanship, not Freedom of Expression, Framed the Case

David Copeland

IN 1735, THE PRINTER JOHN PETER ZENGER stood before the judges of New York's Supreme Court to answer charges of seditious libel brought against him by Gov. William Cosby. It should have been an "open-and-shut" case: for the prosecution to win, it only had to establish that Zenger had printed the newspapers that offended Gov. Cosby's government—something Zenger's lawyer admitted in open court. After a day of testimony and a short jury deliberation, however, the printer was found not guilty of libel. The jury defied the court's instruction and British law with its ruling, and it seemed to say that truth, indeed, negated libel charges.

In the 265-plus years since the verdict, the Zenger trial has assumed a place of importance in understanding the development of freedom of the press in America, in the demand by Americans for the First Amendment to the Constitution and in the courage of printers to fight evil and corrupt government. That is how the writers of America's first media histories wrote of the event and that is how it is remembered by many—even though recent scholarship has complicated the story by properly placing the trial in the context of its times.

The trial of John Peter Zenger had little to do with freedom of the press in colonial America. It had much to do with political control and partisanship in New York. In 1735, freedom of the press served as the means to an end. When political controversies arose and were discussed in newspapers, printers often surrounded potentially volatile articles with essays on the liberty of the press. Printers felt the articles protected them by pointing out the importance of free expression in a free society.

Zenger's trial lawyer, Philadelphia attorney Andrew Hamilton, however, based his defense of the German immigrant printer on the idea that truth negated a charge of libel—even though British law stated that truth made no difference and, indeed, made the libel worse because it could not be refuted. People have a right, Hamilton argued, to criticize their government. The significance of the Zenger trial, then, lies in its proposal in court that truth should be given voice and not punished, an idea that had been debated in America and England since the 17th century, and in the proposal that juries, not judges, should decide whether libels occurred. Even though Hamilton's defense did not change the law, it did become, according to one colonist writing in the *Pennsylvania Gazette* three years later, "better than the law, it ought to be law, and will always be law wherever justice prevails," because the jury recognized its own power and the power of the truth.

In 1733, ZENGER WAS A struggling printer in New York. Like many others in colonial America who had come before him and would come after, he learned his profession as an apprentice. As a "printer's devil" for New York printer William Bradford, Zenger set type and printed on a press that was nearly identical to the one invented by Johannes Gutenberg in 1455. The workday ran according to the sunlight. Lead type was set into frames, locked into the press, inked and pressed onto paper made of cloth. Print shops aimed at producing 250 pressings per hour, and, usually, if this goal could not be met, no one was paid. When Zenger opened his print shop in 1726, he was no rival to his former master, Bradford, the colony's official printer. Bradford received all of the colonial government's printing business, and he published New York's only newspaper, the *Gazette*. Zenger, meanwhile, struggled to make a living by publishing stationery and a variety of pamphlets and books.

The roots of the controversy that sent Zenger to jail for libel were buried deep in the partisan politics of New York, which gained new intensity when Gov. John Montgomerie died in 1731. Naming a new governor was the crown's responsibility, and it often took more than a year for news of a governor's death to reach England and for a new governor to be named and assume office. In the interim, the senior member of the colony's provincial council served as governor; in New York, that was Rip Van Dam, a 72-year-old Anglo-Dutch merchant. Van Dam had been a member of the council for nearly 30 years. Interim governors received governor's pay until the governor arrived from England. Often, the interim set aside half the pay to give to the newly appointed governor, but in Van Dam's case, the council decided that the whole salary should be Van Dam's, probably out of deference to his age, council seniority and service to the colony.

When William Cosby arrived in New York and assumed the governorship, he demanded a pay raise and half of Van Dam's salary. The colony gave the new governor the pay increase, but contrary to custom Van Dam did not surrender half of the pay he had earned as interim governor, a decision initially backed by the council. Gov. Cosby brought suit and arranged for the colony's Supreme Court to sit in judgment of the case.

The move pitted the colony's two political factions against each other. On one side was Gov. Cosby and those who supported him—the Cosby party. On the other side was Chief Justice Lewis Morris and a number of influential people, including lawyers James Alexander and William Smith, who opposed the governor—the Morris party. The two lawyers argued that the court should not hear Cosby's petition. Justice Morris, Cosby's political opponent, naturally, agreed. As a result, Cosby removed Justice Morris from the court, which elevated the controversy to a new level.

The Morris party looked for a way to sway public opinion against Gov. Cosby. Pamphlets and broadsides were possibilities, but letters and essays in a regularly published newspaper, they knew, would be better. Bradford would never print criticism of Cosby in his *Gazette* because it would endanger his status as the colony's official printer, which amounted to a government subsidy. The Morris party thus needed a new newspaper.

When the Morris party contacted Zenger and offered to finance a newspaper for him, he agreed. Zenger (who never truly mastered English and whose spelling of the day of his paper's publication as "Munday" for its entire run stands out even in the idiosyncratic orthography of the 18th century) became the mechanic—the person responsible for overseeing the setting of type and the printing of the *New-York Weekly Journal.* Alexander and Smith served as the editors and chief opinion writers. In the second and third *Weekly Journals,* they inserted an essay on the significance of freedom of the press signed by "Cato," which recalled for New Yorkers the 1720s' English libertarians John Trenchard and Thomas Gordon, who wrote on the rights of Englishmen. Americans often borrowed the name Cato when they wrote on issues that focused on basic rights. From the beginning, then, it appeared that the *Weekly Journal* was about freedom of the press. But espousing press freedom was one way printers in the 18th century protected themselves when political controversy was about to become the central focus of newspaper articles. Many printers espoused impartiality in printing, believing that both sides of issues should be given voice. For some, the rationale for an open press may have been financial; controversy produces increased readership and paper sales. But there was also a growing belief in 18th-century America that all ideas needed to be heard. If printers could be jailed every time a political leader or influential individual believed himself to be slandered in print, printers would lose their livelihood, and Americans would not have an open avenue for discussion. Calls for liberty of the press, therefore, were generally designed to protect printers when their subject matter might be considered controversial, not to champion a concept of freedom of expression that was slowly evolving and would continue to evolve for the next two centuries.

DURING THE NEXT YEAR, the *Weekly Journal* repeatedly attacked Gov. Cosby. It called the governor a French sympathizer for allowing a ship, Le Cæsar, into New York harbor. Britain and France, old enemies, had already fought two wars in North America. The *Weekly Journal* charged that Cosby assisted the French in gaining military information about the city by allowing the ship into the harbor under the pretense of obtaining provisions for starving settlers on Cape Breton. The charge was tantamount to calling the governor a traitor.

A series of unsigned letters in the *Weekly Journal*—a standard 18th-century practice to protect the writers, along with the use of pseudonyms—attacked abuses of power by Gov. Cosby's administration. When the Cosby party complained, Alexander and Smith inserted more of Cato's letters on the value of freedom of the press in the *Weekly Journal.* "Whoever would overthrow the Liberty of the Nation," the paper declared, "must begin by subduing the Freeness of Speech; A Thing terrible to publick Traytors."

By November 1734, Gov. Cosby had had enough of the attacks in the *Weekly Journal.* He ordered four particularly offensive issues of the paper confiscated and burned in public. The next week, the *Weekly Journal* boldly proclaimed, "Only the wicked Governours of Men dread what is said of them."

Gov. Cosby immediately signed orders for Zenger's arrest for seditious libel, which meant he printed material that undermined the authority of government. The paper missed its next publication because Zenger was in jail. At his hearing, the court set Zenger's bail at £400. Zenger could not afford the excessive bail, but the wealthy Morris party could. They chose, however, to leave Zenger behind bars: he was worth more as a martyr to the harsh practices of a tyrannical governor than as a printer. Zenger remained in jail until his August trial, but the paper continued to publish with Zenger's wife, Anna, and apprentices doing the work.

Although the Morris party would not bail Zenger out of jail, it did intend to provide him with counsel in court. Alexander and Smith planned to represent the printer; they began Zenger's defense by questioning the impartiality of two judges sitting on the court to hear the case because both were staunch supporters of Cosby. As a result of their petition to have the two recused from the case, Alexander and Smith were disbarred. The court appointed another lawyer, John Chambers, who held a government job thanks to an appointment from Cosby, to defend Zenger.

To Chamber's credit, he fought a plan to have the jury in the case chosen from a list of Cosby party members. Instead, Chambers successfully insisted that the jury be chosen from all eligible New York landowners. Chambers' persistence for a nonpartial jury probably made as much difference as the defense presented by Hamilton. At trial, all the prosecution needed to do was prove that Zenger published the material considered libelous. If the jury affirmed that fact, Zenger would then be judged guilty.

When it came time for Zenger's defense, it was not Chambers who rose in the courtroom but Andrew Hamilton. Hamilton was considered by most to be the best trial lawyer in the colonies. When Alexander and Smith were disbarred, they contacted Hamilton about assuming the role of counsel for Zenger when the printer went to court. The 59-

year-old Hamilton admitted that Zenger printed the tracts in question, but he did not stop there. He said that lack of governmental approval did not necessarily make a publication libelous and then added two significant points. First, Hamilton said a jury and not a judge should decide the libelous nature of material. Second, and contrary to the chief justice's instructions, he insinuated that truth negated libel. "They are notoriously known to be true," Hamilton said of the facts surrounding the *Weekly Journal*'s accusations to the jury. "Therefore in your justice lies our safety."

The jury ensured Zenger his safety and found him not guilty after deliberating for only a short time. Zenger was freed and went back to publishing the *Weekly Journal.* Two years later, the Morris party gained control of the New York political machinery with a convincing victory at the polls. Zenger's effort in helping Morris, Alexander, Smith, Van Dam and others in their fight against Gov. Cosby's administration was not forgotten. Zenger became the colony's official printer, with all the access to government printing jobs that the position entailed.

FUTURE GENERATIONS WOULD FIND the story of the Zenger case a significant chapter in the story of freedom. While the Zenger trial may have reflected growing American thought on the role of the press and on libel, it did not spark an immediate reaction in the colonial press. Only a few brief statements may be found in papers other than those of New York concerning the controversy. Alexander's and Smith's disbarment, for example, found its way into two newspapers, but Zenger's name was never mentioned. The trial's results appeared only in Zenger's newspaper and in a pamphlet that he himself published. Discussion of the trial in the press did not occur until 1737 and 1738 when the decision was attacked by a writer in a Barbados paper and the *Pennsylvania Gazette* printed responses.

And what happened in Zenger's court case did not immediately change the law concerning libel. Even though the case became a major topic of discussion in England in the years after the trial, British law did not give juries the power to decide libel cases until 1792 and did not recognize truth as a libel defense until 1843. New York law did not validate truth as a libel defense until 1821.

The verdict in the Zenger trial did, however, echo growing sentiment in America that people had the right to criticize their government and that using courts to punish printers or anyone else who did so was improper. Few printers from 1735 on in colonial America faced seditious libel charges. In revolutionary-minded Boston from 1765 on, crown-appointed leaders were continually vilified in print, but no charges of seditious libel could ever be obtained. As legal historian Leonard Levy pointed out, "The law of seditious libel simply had no meaning any longer."

The trial of John Peter Zenger has been proclaimed as an example of courage in which a single printer faced the powerful political machinery of the time and remained in jail for the honor of freedom of the press. Zenger, of course, did not want to stay imprisoned; he simply had no choice. This does not mean that courage was not a part of the story. Gov. Cosby knew that Alexander and Smith were writing the inflammatory letters about him, but the governor could not prove it since nothing in the *Weekly Journal* was signed. Only Zenger's name appeared on the newspaper. And Zenger had to know that arrest for printing the letters that attacked the governor was possible; his mentor, the printer Bradford who ultimately sided with the Court party, had once been jailed in Pennsylvania for printing views contrary to the government's. Bradford surely told Zenger this story as the young immigrant worked as Bradford's apprentice.

Zenger's paper offended not just the governor but his supporters. One of Cosby's staunchest devotees on the provincial council, Francis Harison, threatened to beat Zenger if he caught him on the streets. Zenger took the threat seriously and began to wear a sword in public. Alexander and Smith also lived under a threat they presumed to be from Harison, who was assigned by the governor to write pro-Cosby articles for the *Gazette*. In an unsigned note left on Alexander's door in February 1734 were the words, "I swear by God to poison all your tribe so surely, that you shan't know the perpetrator of the tragedy." Alexander and Smith believed Harison wrote the warning, even though the council said that Harison was incapable of such deeds.

The Zenger trial was but one of the many political power struggles that took place in colonial America. Those in power generally supported stricter press control; that is why Cosby clamped down on the *Weekly Journal* and that is why, during the 1770s patriots used boycotts, intimidation and outright violence to silence Tory printers, even as both groups of printers championed freedom of the press from the pages of their newspapers. A fear of power in a national government led to the Bill of Rights. Even though Zenger's trial was never mentioned during the debates surrounding the Constitution or the First Amendment, perhaps the trial—or what the trial said about truth, libel and printing—had somehow become a part of America's consciousness. Surely newspapers had become a part of the fabric of American life. Perhaps, too, episodes such as that of the trial of John Peter Zenger unwittingly paved the way for freedom of the press and even pluralism because they helped acclimate people to a society where political dispute and criticism became commonplace.

David Copeland is an associate professor of mass communication at Emory & Henry College and author of Colonial American Newspapers: Character and Content and Debating the Issues in Colonial Newspapers.

2

David Ruggles

The Hazards of Anti-Slavery Journalism

Graham Russell Hodges

ABOLITIONISTS ORGANIZING THE battle against slavery during the 1830s quickly mastered the potentials of the penny press and the post office in their campaign to compel Americans to examine their consciences about the South's "peculiar institution." The movement published millions of broadsides and introduced fiery newspapers advancing the cause. Its emotional exhortations convinced thousands of ordinary Americans to voice their anger at human bondage by sending nearly a million petitions through the mails, beseeching Congress to abolish slavery. Federal legislators had already passed a gag rule prohibiting such discussion. Former President John Quincy Adams, now a congressman, often raised the petitions on the floor, forcing opponents into embarrassing stipulations to table the letters. Undeterred anti-slavery citizens continued the cascade of pleas against any enlargement of the servile system. The movement survived violence, too, when anti-abolitionist rioters burned presses and killed one editor in Illinois in 1837. White editors William Lloyd Garrison and David Lee Child are widely known for their brave commitment to abolitionist publishing. Other than Frederick Douglass, far less is known about the courageous black journalists who strived to extinguish slavery.

David Ruggles, an African-American printer in New York City during the 1830s, was the prototype for black activist journalists of his

11

time. During his 20-year career, Ruggles poured out hundreds of articles, published at least five pamphlets and operated the first African-American press. His magazine, *Mirror of Liberty*, intermittently issued between 1838 and 1841, is widely recognized as the first periodical published by a black American. Ruggles also displayed unyielding courage against constant violence, which eventually destroyed his health and career. His story reveals the valor required of a black editor struggling against the pitiless hatred of the pro-slavery forces and the yawning indifference of most Americans. Ruggles' valiant work ran the spectrum of the work of journalists. He was an agent, writer, printer, publisher and subject. He was in fact America's first black working journalist. His career epitomized the fusion of professionalism and activism, so characteristic of later black journalists, that would propel him to the center of racial conflict.

RUGGLES WAS BORN IN NORWICH, Connecticut, in 1810, the eldest of seven children of free black parents. His father, David Sr., was a blacksmith. His mother, Nancy, was a noted caterer and a founding member of the local Methodist church. Ruggles was educated at religious charity schools in Norwich. By the age of 17, he was in New York, first working as a mariner; in 1828 he opened a grocery shop. At first he sold liquor. Observing, as did other black abolitionists, the damage done to the black community by drink, he converted to the temperance movement. He advocated it in his advertisements in *Freedom's Journal*, the nation's first black newspaper, which was published by Samuel Eli Cornish, a black Presbyterian minister.

By the early 1830s, Ruggles became involved in the growing antislavery movement in New York. White radicals, disenchanted by reform measures, now joined blacks demanding the immediate end of slavery. His grocery shop at 1 Cortlandt Street was the nation's first black bookstore until a mob destroyed it. In 1833, the *Emancipator*, an abolitionist weekly, appointed him as its agent to canvass for subscribers throughout the Middle Atlantic states. By 1834, Ruggles was also writing regularly. That year, he published his own pamphlet entitled The "Extinguisher" Extinguished: or David M. Reese, M.D. "Used Up..." a satirical screed attacking the leading local proponent of the American Colonization Society. This organization, which roused fiery anger in Ruggles and other blacks, argued that the only solution for America's racial problems was to ship all free blacks to Africa. However implausible this sounds today, the plan was very popular among whites in the antebellum United States. Yet blacks understood, Ruggles thundered, that the plan did not threaten the future of slavery. His self-published booklet was the first imprint by an African American.

Ruggles used his own press the next year in his publication Abrogation of the seventh commandment, by the American Churches, which contended that Northern white women should shun their Southern sisters, whom, he argued, acquiesced in the violation of God's commandments by letting their husbands keep enslaved black women as mistresses. Ruggles beseeched Northern women to consider whether they would "tolerate the adoption of a system which would recognize as their domestic servant the spurious off-spring of their own husbands, brothers, and sons." He lashed out at Southern women as "inexcusably criminal" for disregarding the sexual exploitation of enslaved black women. Ruggles' jeremiad foreshadowed similar developments in the nascent feminist movement and revealed growing personal splits between North and South.

Ruggles believed deeply that newspapers were necessary tools of anyone opposed to the evil of slavery. He enunciated his beliefs in a series of six articles published in the *Emancipator* early in 1835. Ruggles was worried that a lack of subscriptions from blacks might doom anti-slavery journalism. He urged African Americans to do their duty by supporting the *Emancipator* and other anti-slavery journals because they were the most effective weapons against servitude. In a nation where few blacks could vote and none could hold office, he remarked, freedom of the press was blacks' most precious liberty. Costing only a few cents a copy, the newspapers were an essential and inexpensive means to combat slavery. For blacks to ignore their "trumpets of freedom" was to display the personal degradation of enslavement. No one in America, he contended with remarkable prescience, could be neutral on the moral issue of slavery. Blacks and sympathetic whites had a moral obligation to support abolitionist newspapers.

RUGGLES RAISED MORE than his pen in his personal war against the slavocracy. In 1835, he and several other young black activists organized the New York Committee of Vigilance. Manhattan was then swarming with "kidnappers," agents of Southern slave owners whose chattel had fled north to freedom. With the help of New York City magistrates, kidnappers seized blacks off the street, held a quick hearing to "prove" their identity and within a matter of hours forced their unfortunate victims onto boats headed for Southern ports. Angered by this practice, Ruggles and the rest of the Committee of Vigilance openly confronted slave catchers, demanded that the city government grant jury trials to fugitives and offered legal assistance to them. Backed by the New York Manumission Society, whose members included the lawyer William Jay, son of Chief Justice John Jay, the Committee of Vigilance proved highly effective in protecting the rights of local blacks. On several occasions, Ruggles went to private homes where enslaved blacks were hidden and informed the servants that they were actually free. In case anyone missed these activities, Ruggles often published such adventures in abolitionist newspapers such as the *Emancipator* and the *Liberator*.

One of Ruggles' most controversial methods was to demand the arrest of white sea captains he suspected of trading in slaves. Illegal since 1808, slave trading still occurred clandestinely. Ruggles' unmasking of these transactions nearly cost him his freedom.

In December 1836, a Portuguese vessel captained by Juan Evangelista de Souza arrived in New York harbor. Ruggles heard from wharfside sources that the captain held five blacks in slavery and intended to head south to sell them. Under a writ of habeas corpus, Ruggles demanded that the five enslaved blacks be held in a local jail until a hearing could be held on their status. He also sought successfully the arrest of Captain de Souza on charges of slave trading. This was the second time Ruggles had a white man arrested on such charges. His boldness infuriated his opponents. While the case wound through the courts, de Souza, who was free on bail, and a local police officer named Tobias Boudinot and a slave catcher named D.D. Nash decided to take matters into their own hands. Late on the night of December 28, 1836, they arrived at Ruggles' home at 67 Lispenard Street. They knocked loudly and asked to speak to David. When Ruggles told them to come back in the morning, they tried to break down his door. Ruggles escaped and returned later with a watchman. At a hearing at the police station, Ruggles exposed his assailants' plot to grab him and put him on a vessel headed for Savannah, Georgia, where he would be sold into slavery. Frustrated, Nash tried to arrest Ruggles on a specious writ for any black who looked like Jesse or Abraham, generic names for slaves. If it hadn't been for the help of his white allies among local lawyers, Ruggles doubtless would have been shipped off into slavery. Sometime later, Nash proclaimed—during a mobbing of a white abolitionist named John Hopper in Savannah—that he would give "a thousand dollars if he had that nigger named Ruggles in my hands as he is the leader of [the abolitionists]."

Undeterred by these threats, Ruggles continued to publish his articles and pamphlets, writing dozens of pieces for newspapers throughout the Northeast. He was also the most visible conductor on the Underground Railroad. Ruggles claimed to have helped 400 fugitive slaves during the 1830s. One such escaped slave later became one of the most famous Americans of the 19th century. In his classic autobiography, Frederick Douglass recalled his dire straits just after he fled north to freedom in New York City in late September 1838. Though exhilarated by his newfound freedom, Douglass was terrified of slave catchers. The young fugitive was broke, lonely and spent several nights sleeping amidst empty barrels on the wharves. Fortunately, he met a sailor who took him to the print shop of David Ruggles, who sheltered him and welcomed him to freedom with great celebration. A few days later, Frederick was married to Anna Murray, a free black woman, in Ruggles' shop in a ceremony led by James W.C. Pennington, a former fugitive turned Presbyterian minister. Immediately after the wedding, Douglass and his new wife traveled to New Bedford, Massachusetts, armed with a letter of recommendation from Ruggles and a $5 bill. In just a few years Douglass became one of America's most famous abolitionist orators. Today, his autobiography is read by tens of thousands of college students and is considered a classic of American literature.

BY THE TIME DOUGLASS met him, Ruggles had become one of the most notorious black abolitionists in the United States. A look at a remarkable incident, which took place right around the time Douglass arrived in New York City, reveals the energy and courage demanded of Ruggles as he used his pen and life to fight against slavery. The Darg Case, as it was called, caused a furor in New York's newspapers in the autumn of 1838. Its proceeding exposed the extreme dangers for Ruggles and other anti-slavery warriors.

New York City residents in the 1830s were deeply divided over the future of America's peculiar institution. It was naturally abhorred by the city's 16,000 black residents, many of whom had been only recently emancipated by legislative decree ending slavery in New York state in 1827. Much of the city's elite also worked against it, though by different means. Some elite urbanites favored the strategy of the American Colonization Society, with its plan of sending free blacks back to Africa. Others, notably the Jay family, preferred black self-help efforts at home and donated money to the New York Manumission Society and its principal agency, the African Free School. Though the school had declined recently, it was the alma mater of the city's black elite. A more radical wing of the Manumission Society sided with "immediatists"—anti-slavery activists such as William Lloyd Garrison and the Tappan brothers, founders of Dun and Bradstreet—who wanted slavery ended now, not later.

One of the most active Manumission Society members with this view was Barney Corse, who, for more than 10 years, had helped self-emancipated or fugitive slaves come north and helped local blacks protect their freedom against kidnappers. Joining him was the venerable Isaac T. Hopper, a Quaker abolitionist since the 1780s, and Ruggles. This trio had successfully battled city officials and kidnappers on several occasions. At other times, when they lost, Ruggles used his press to blast this unfair system. Some situations were uncomplicated; others, such as the Darg Case, were complex. The facts, as they came out in the subsequent trial, were as follows: On August 25, 1838, John P. Darg, a Virginia slaveholder, arrived in New York City with his slave Thomas Hughes. The issue of Southerners bringing their human chattel to a free state was under intense negotiation between the governors of New York and Virginia, but Darg apparently felt confident about the status of his servant. But a few days later Hughes came to Hopper's house, seeking refuge. The Quaker, however, was initially reluctant and asked Hughes to leave his home. The next day, the *New York Sun*, the most vitriolic of the penny press, published a notice offering a reward for the return of Hughes and the $7,000 or $8,000 he had taken with him. Hopper, Corse and perhaps Ruggles served as go-betweens for Darg and Hughes. The slave no longer had all the money, having given some of it to others who helped him escape and a portion to some local gamblers.

Corse and Ruggles decided that returning the cash was moral but turning over Hughes was not. They convinced Darg to free Hughes provided that he gave back as much money as he took. When the sum turned out to be far less than Darg demanded, the slave master ordered Corse and Ruggles arrested for grand larceny. Corse quickly found bail, but Ruggles was jailed for two days with common criminals, even though he had not actually been charged with anything. After that incident, a caricature of the three, entitled "The Disappointed Abolitionists," was published, suggesting that they were really interested in the reward and, rather than trying to free slaves, were setting up an extortion ring to prey on unwary masters.

The case remained newsworthy over the next few months. In October, a group of black citizens honored Ruggles by giving him a cane with a golden knob. Sadly, the struggle was taking its toll on the valiant Ruggles. Now only 28 years old, he was nearly blind and was afflicted with severe bowel disorders. All of his money and time went into the movement, so he often was homeless. Worse afflictions were on the way, and they came from a surprising source.

IN 1837, SAMUEL ELI CORNISH, aided by Philip A. Bell, resurrected his black newspaper and renamed it the *Colored American*. Ruggles quickly became a regular contributor. The editors in turn frequently wrote approvingly of his actions. But in early 1839, a terrible dispute arose that ended Ruggles' career in New York City. Hearing rumors that a black hotelier named John Russell was hiding captive blacks before they were transported south, Ruggles, without Cornish's knowledge, inserted an article in the *Colored American* accusing the innkeeper of helping kidnappers. Russell sued the newspaper, Ruggles and Cornish for libel and won a judgment of $600—which nearly bankrupted the weekly journal. Furious, Cornish attacked Ruggles in print. Although wealthy benefactors soon paid the libel award, Cornish campaigned to have Ruggles driven out of the movement. One method was to demand that Ruggles explain every cash expenditure of the Committee of Vigilance. After a careful accounting, it appeared that the committee's funds were short $400. Broken in health and deeply hurt by Cornish's accusations, Ruggles was forced to resign his post as secretary of the committee. Before doing so, he published his last imprint in New York City, *A Plea for a Man and a Brother,* in which he tried to refute Cornish's indictments. In truth, the more conservative Cornish and his many allies had tired of Ruggles' radical methods and sought less confrontational means to fight slavery.

Although he still published regularly in white abolitionist journals, Ruggles' plight was desperate. Now blind and seriously ill from several diseases, he left New York for Massachusetts. His father died in

1841. Fearful that Ruggles might soon follow him to the grave, William C. Nell and other Boston blacks honored the ailing man with a dinner and a gift of badly needed funds. They proclaimed him a great soldier in the war against slavery. That winter, noted author Lydia Maria Child and her husband, David Lee Child, editor of the *National Anti-Slavery Standard*, arranged for Ruggles to join a radical commune in Northampton, Massachusetts. Ruggles, grateful for their help and anxious to find a cure for his many ailments, became first an adherent and later a doctor of hydropathy, a water cure regimen then sweeping the nation. By 1845, Ruggles established the first water cure hospital in the United States. He continued writing a dozen or more articles on abolitionism annually as well as publishing in water-cure journals. Just as his new career soared to new heights, Ruggles tragically succumbed to a severe bowel infection on December 18, 1849. His family came to retrieve his body and buried him in their plot in Norwich. As the anti-slavery movement mourned Ruggles, William Lloyd Garrison summarized his many achievements and plaintively noted "his biography is yet to be written." One hundred fifty years later, that fact is still true, but Ruggles may be remembered for his fusion of committed journalism and fearless activism.

Graham Russell Hodges, professor of history at Colgate University, is the author of Root and Branch: African Americans in New York and East Jersey, 1613-1863. *He is writing a biography of David Ruggles.*

3

Francisco P. Ramírez

Californio Editor and Yanqui Conquest

Félix Gutiérrez

LESS THAN A DECADE AFTER Los Angeles residents had seen the border between the United States and Mexico redrawn to leave them inside the United States, Californios had become strangers in their own land. Left between two nations and two cultures, they found themselves living in an Anglo system they did not understand and that, in turn, showed little desire to understand them or their Latino ways.

The efforts to find ways to combine Anglo and Hispanic cultures go on today, as Hispanics continue to grow in the U.S. population and are projected to be the nation's largest racial or ethnic minority group within four years.

Like other Latinos left north of the border in 1848, Californios were among the first to face the realities of being Latino in an Anglo world. They looked for guidance. Some found it in the words of Francisco P. Ramírez, teen-age editor of the first Spanish-language newspaper of Los Angeles, *El Clamor Público* (The Public Outcry). In his May 10, 1856, edition, he wrote, "California has fallen into the hands of the ambitious sons of North America, who will not stop until they have satisfied their passions, by driving the first occupants of the land out of the country, vilifying their religion and disfiguring their customs."

Like many educated Californios, Ramírez first welcomed the ideals of equality, democracy and civil liberties espoused in the U.S. Consti-

19

tution. But he was disappointed when his people and their rights were trampled upon by the Yanquis espousing those ideals. Nevertheless he tried to take the best from both worlds, finding his own democratic thinking was best reflected in the Republican Party ideals of the day.

"The North Americans pretend to give us lessons in humanity and to bring to our people the doctrine of salvation so we can govern ourselves, to respect the laws and conserve order. Are these the ones who treat us worse than slaves?" he wrote in a September 1855 article condemning lynchings of Mexicanos.

The lynchings, squatters and imposition of a new language, culture and legal system made the years following the United States-Mexico War of 1846 to 1848 violent and unpleasant for Spanish-speaking residents in the lands stretching from Arkansas and Louisiana west to the Pacific Ocean and as far north as Wyoming. In the name of Manifest Destiny, the United States had waged a war of conquest to acquire these territories and the prized San Francisco Bay as its Pacific outpost. A new international boundary was drawn, extending more than 2,000 miles from near San Diego eastward to the Rio Grande and thence to the Gulf of Mexico. The lands north of this line eventually became all or part of the states of California, Texas, Nevada, Utah, Colorado, New Mexico, Arizona, Kansas, Oklahoma and Wyoming.

But along with the mountains, prairies and deserts came thousands of Tejanos in Texas, Hispanos in New Mexico and Californios in California who found themselves on the Yanqui side of a changed border. They had not come to the United States. The United States had come to them. And it had arrived in the form of battleships and invading armies. U.S. treaty negotiators promised their Mexican counterparts that the rights of former Mexican citizens would be respected. But the U.S. Senate canceled provisions in the Treaty of Guadalupe Hidalgo enumerating those rights. The result: a victorious minority was in power over a vanquished majority.

This United States military conquest, which followed earlier economic penetration of the Mexican territories, was itself followed by efforts to dominate the majority native populations politically, socially and culturally. The signing of the Treaty of Guadalupe Hidalgo signaled the end of military action but the beginning of domestic cycles of conquest.

MANY ANGLOS CAME WEST by ship or covered wagon infused with a desire to exploit natural resources that had been held by people who they felt did not deserve them. Richard Henry Dana's 1840 book, *Two Years Before the Mast*, portrayed the Californios as too lazy to develop their own lands and, noting the good climate and harbor, said that "nothing but the character of the people prevents Monterey from becoming a great town." Four years later Illinois lawyer and travel writer Thomas Jefferson Farnham observed in a book on his California travels, "The Californios are an imbecile, pusillanimous race of men, and unfit to control the destinies of that beautiful country." The words of U.S. journalists were just as harsh.

"What has miserable, inefficient Mexico, with her superstition, her burlesque upon freedom, her actual tyranny by the few over the many— what has she to do with the great mission of peopling the new world with a noble race? Be it ours, to achieve that mission!" Walt Whitman wrote in the *Brooklyn Eagle* during the war.

After the war some parts of the former Mexican department of Alta California changed more quickly than others. Following the 1848 discovery of gold in the Sierra Nevada foothills east of present-day Sacramento, thousands of gold seekers converged from around the world to quickly build up the city of San Francisco and establish mining camps in the gold fields. Californios and Native Americans were the targets of vigilantes, lynchings and violence as Anglos took their homes, lands and possessions.

But in pastoral southern California, ranching and agricultural pursuits dominated. There the Californios predominated numerically for a longer time as a slower stream of Anglo settlers entered the newly acquired territories with their own institutions, including the press. Change came more slowly than in the north, but ultimately with no less impact.

SEVERAL NEWSPAPERS HAD BEEN PUBLISHED in Texas and New Mexico before the war with the United States. But while California printer Augustín Zamorano had set up a print shop in Monterey in 1834, apparently no Californio took up his offer to provide "equitable prices with gentlemen who may wish to establish any periodical." In the years following the war, journalism flourished in both Spanish and English in the territories taken from Mexico. One directory lists 132

Spanish-language or bilingual newspapers published between 1848 and 1900 in what had become the southwestern United States.

Many were financed by political parties or business interests that linked them to the new power structure. In fact, in keeping with the Treaty of Guadalupe Hidalgo, some newspapers received government subsidies for printing laws and public notices bilingually or in Spanish.

Los Angeles' first newspaper, the *Los Angeles Star*, began in 1851 as a bilingual newspaper receiving a state subsidy to print laws in Spanish. The four-page paper devoted its back section to *La Estrella de Los Angeles:* Spanish-language news, advertising and public notices.

Out of that section evolved *El Clamor Público* in June 1855, edited by teen-ager Ramírez, who had been a compositor and one in a string of editors of *La Estrella.* The value of Ramírez's work had been noted in February 1855 by San Francisco's English-language daily the *Alta California,* which observed, "Those versed in the Castilian language say that *La Estrella* is a model for purity of style."

Born in Los Angeles in 1837 and with no formal education except for a year studying in San José, Ramírez left the Star to begin *El Clamor Público* "because he had to handle copy tinged with a seemingly repellent gringo chauvinism," wrote Leonard Pitt in *The Decline of the Californios.* So he began Los Angeles' third newspaper and the first one to be printed mainly in Spanish. The weekly went to press on Thursday and sold at $5 a year.

By the end of May 1855, "the *Star* had given up all its Spanish-language news and advertisements. The paper transferred them to *El Clamor Público,* a journal which was to be 'devoted exclusively to the service and interests of Native Californians,'" wrote William B. Rice in his book, *The Los Angeles Star.* Ramírez, described by Rice as "a precocious Angeleno and multilinguist," announced the birth of the new paper in the Star, noting that 100 subscribers would be needed to begin publication.

"Today we respectfully greet the public," Ramírez wrote in an opening editorial that noted Anglo interest in his newspaper. "We ask our patrons for the liberal subscriptions they have favored us with. Even though it is difficult to say, the foreigners have demonstrated much more fervor in subscribing to the paper than the Californios themselves."

El Clamor Público started out with a moderate, businesslike tone. It was a five-column paper, smaller than its two competitors, and with few advertisements at first. That number later grew. Advertising and subscription rates were the same as for the Star, $2 and $5 respectively. Publishing many poems, it said in its masthead that it was a "Periódico Independiente y Literaria." Like the *Star, El Clamor Público* benefited from printing contracts with local and state officials, sometimes printing a law in Spanish for the city and publishing ordinances and official notices for the state.

ALONG WITH SOME LEADING Californios, Ramírez embraced the liberal ideas discussed in other Western nations of his time. In June 1855, he wrote that the paper was dedicated to "political independence," "moral and material progress" and a "regime of law and order." He supported the "magnanimous and grandiose ideals" of the U.S. Constitution and Declaration of Independence and the nation's dedication to popular government, economic progress, civil rights and the "arts of peace."

Taking the founding fathers at their word and then experiencing the offenses committed against his people, however, Ramírez soon struck a more courageous editorial tone.

"El Clamor nicely captured the distressed mood of the Latin Americans of southern California; it gave them remarkably good news coverage and a public forum for their ideals," wrote Pitt. "If Manuel Reytes felt outraged by the Yankee's selfish use of the word 'American,' he could write a dissertation urging that the 'sacrosanct' term should embrace all people of the Western Hemisphere—Latin Americans as well as Anglo Americans. If the anonymous writer signing himself 'Consistencia' wished to dilate on the gringo legal profession and publicly swear off ever voting for a lawyer again, or if 'Uno Mexicano' wished simply to unburden himself generally about the assorted miseries of his people in California, the columns of *El Clamor Público* were open and waiting."

Ramírez, Pitt wrote, "for four years from 1855 to 1859 was the new self-styled champion of the Spanish Americans in California. A good deal of his fervor, bombast, and eloquence stemmed from his youth and his awareness of the difficulties of the younger generation. A baby when his elders were fighting rebellions, a boy during the gold rush, a youth who had neither land or cattle, nor stature in the better classes, Ramírez, nevertheless, somehow managed to articulate the views of most Californios in the 1850s."

Ramírez's commitment to civil liberties often irritated the *Star*. The *Star* even accused him of exaggerating the Californio's plight and stirring up racial hatreds.

Ramírez also kept an eye on the Star, complaining when that newspaper reported the "tendencies of our Mexican population toward armed riot, scuffling and robbery." Ramírez commented that it was unfair to insult all Mexicans via the "depraved imagination" of the *Star* and thanked the better classes of Norteamericanos for being more fair-minded.

El Clamor Público's coverage, Pitt has written, went far beyond the news of the day. Its editorials condemned lynching, embraced a wide range of reforms, denounced filibusterers and squatters, and encouraged Californios to better their lives by emigrating to the Sonora region of northern Mexico. It also published poetry in Spanish and reviews.

Ramírez did not stand apart from the debates over slavery that increasingly gripped politics in the United States. In fact, his hostility to slavery propelled him into the Republican Party when it emerged in the 1850s with a platform of opposition to the spread of human bondage to the west.

"His outlook, his journalistic techniques were very American," says Claremont, California, attorney Paul Gray, who is preparing a history journal article on Ramírez. "He was a courageous person. From 1855 to 1859 he was an anti-slavery Republican governed by the principles of Mexican liberalism. He believed in racial equality for Indians, Chinese and Negroes."

El Clamor Público reflected and disseminated the open-minded views of liberal thinkers of the times. Ramírez advocated public education for all, including girls, so they would not be infantile or ignorant playthings of their husbands.

IN A REGION DOMINATED by southern Chivalry Democrats, who brought the prevailing racial attitudes of the Cotton Kingdom with them when they migrated to California, *El Clamor Público* became one of the few Republican newspapers. Its advocacy on behalf of African Americans caused the *San Francisco Herald* to label it the most violent of all the "Free Nigger organs" in the state during the 1856 elections. Ramírez opposed extension of slavery to new territories, such as California, and slavery itself. He also fought proposed laws limiting the rights of free Negroes in the state.

Debates over slavery and the rights of African Americans compounded arguments about the place of Mexicans in the new California.
Some Californios, especially the gente de razón, who considered themselves Spanish and identified with the upper classes, favored adoption
of the Anglo traditions and culture. But the lower-class cholos and
mestizos often preferred defiance or, at least, retention of their Hispanic traditions and cultures. Ramírez was sometimes caught in the
middle.

"Elite Mexicans couldn't accept him because he was too radical,"
Gray says. "The Mexican working class didn't accept him because he
was literate and exhorted them to vote and to stand up for their rights.
He was the perennial outsider."

As Rodolfo Acuña observed in *Occupied America*, with the passage
of time Ramírez became more outspoken in criticizing the newcomers.
An August 1855 editorial observed, "World history tells us that the
Anglo-Saxons were in the beginning thieves and pirates the same as
other nations in their infancy . . . [but] the pirate instinct of old Anglo-
Saxons is still active."

Especially prized were California land titles, which took on a major
importance in the gold rush of 1849 and its aftermath. Spanish and
Mexican authorities had made 813 land grants in California. Unlike
grantees in other parts of the newly acquired territories, Californios
were required to defend their titles before a special federal land commission appointed in 1851 and, sometimes, federal district courts and
the U.S. Supreme Court. Squatters, land swindlers and crafty lawyers
steadily whittled away at Californios' land holdings during the pro-
longed and expensive proceedings. When titles were confirmed, successful grantees often had to give up their land to pay the attorneys or
to reimburse squatters for improvements made on their property. "When
they receive patent, if they are not already ruined, they will be very
close to it," *El Clamor Público* complained on August 15, 1857.

From the beginning Ramírez advised those unhappy with the new
conditions to cross the new border and help colonize northern Mexico.
After one reader criticized the "Back to Mexico" stance and implied
that Mexicans were better off than before, Ramírez asked, "Are the
Californios as happy today as when they belonged to the Republic of
Mexico, in spite of all of its revolutions and changes in government?"

His frustrations grew as injustices increased. "Oh! Fatalidad!" pro-
tested an August 1856 *El Clamor Público* editorial: "Mexicans alone

have been the victims of the peoples' insane fury! Mexicans alone
have been sacrificed on the gibbet and launched into eternity...! This is
the liberty and equality of our adopted land! Examine the state's history since the discovery of gold and one must conclude that 'California is lost to all Spanish-Americans.'"

Such editorial crusading irritated at least one Anglo who considered
himself a friend of the Californios. In 1857, Los Angeles Assemblyman Joseph Lancaster Brent said *El Clamor Público* was "disseminat-
ing sentiments of treason and antipathy among the native population."
Ramírez struck back editorially, asking if it was treason to describe
the "tremors of 'a thousand hearts . . . a thousand eyes filled with
tears . . . a thousand hands' of the Californios who see their fathers
and brothers tortured in the presence of innocent children?"

RAMÍREZ ALIGNED HIMSELF with liberal political figures in Latin America,
such as Mexico's President Ignacio Comonfort, whose political attitudes he thought would offer Mexicans on the U.S. side of the border
renewed inspiration to cope with their own lives. *El Clamor Público*
carried much news from Mexico and covered festivities such as the
1855 Mexican Independence Day in Los Angeles.

He also tried to bridge the two worlds that collided in the lives of
his readers, reflecting both the language, culture and interests of the
Latin Americans who had dominated California until 1848 and also
the history and principles of the Anglo-American minority that came
into power after the war. When there were clashes, he reported them
and editorialized on behalf of those he felt were right, be they Anglo
or Californio. And when there was something helpful to be learned
from the newcomers, he passed that along also.

"In many ways Ramírez's evolution reflected that of many
Californios and Mexicans," Acuña wrote. "Once the annexation of
California became a reality, they sincerely sought to become good
citizens; however, when it became evident that they were not considered or treated like first-class citizens, they turned to separatism. Atroci-
ties committed against the Mexican population intimidated and alienated them."

But, as Acuña noted elsewhere, Ramírez did not place all blame on
the Anglos. He called upon his own people to learn to deal with the
newcomers on their own terms and demand their rights. And, as time
went on, he exhorted those who stayed to learn the ways of the con-
queror and use the new system for their own benefit.

"And you, imbecile Californios! You are to blame for the lamentations that we are witnessing. We are tired of saying: open your eyes, and it is time that we demand our rights and interests. It is with shame that we say, and difficult to confess it: you are the sarcasm of humanity!" Ramírez chastised his readers for not voting and for putting up with indignities. Until they cared, they would never cast off the "yoke of slavery," he warned in December 1858.

Ramírez struck an even more strident tone in a June 18, 1859, editorial in English that said "we are Native California Americans born on the soil and we can exclaim with the Poet, this is 'our own, our native land.'" Noting that they were now under the American flag "and there is every probability that we shall remain so for all time to come . . . let us divest ourselves of all bygone traditions, and become Americanized all over—in language, in manners, in customs and in habits." To fail to do so would continue the oppression and victimization the Californios had suffered. For lack of understanding the Anglo ways, "[W]e have seen our countrymen . . . fleeced out of their flocks and herds, ranches and money by cunning 'sharpers' who have taken advantage of their simplicity and their verdancy." The best way to learn, the entrepreneurial Ramírez advised, was to subscribe to *El Clamor Público* and read its renewed English-language page. Noting that a free press was the best guarantee of liberty, Ramírez promised that his paper would "uphold the Constitution of the United States, [being] convinced that only through it will we obtain liberty."

Along with his editorial advocacy, Ramírez pursued his own political agenda. In the 1859 election, the newspaper publicized Republican candidates such as Leland Stanford for governor. Ramírez himself ran a losing second race for the assembly on the Republican ticket. He said he was requested by the "People" to be a candidate for assemblyman in the September 1859 election and used the paper to advocate his candidacy. Several months after his defeat he advertised his printing equipment for sale.

The last issue of *El Clamor Público* appeared on December 31, 1859. Although Ramírez had worked in both the editorial and printing departments to decrease expenses, the *Star* said its end was due entirely to lack of financial resources. Ramírez had tried to forestall its financial demise by appealing for support based on its services to the Republican Party, asking Republican friends throughout the state to collect and send in subscriptions. The *Star* said its competitor was a well-conducted journal, whose indiscretions were linked to Ramírez's youth to which "may be attributed the heated and injudicious attacks on the American government and people which from time to time have appeared in the paper."

After closing the paper, Ramírez took his own editorial advice and moved south to Ures, Sonora, Mexico, where he was editor of *La Estrella de Occidente* and director of public printing for the state. In 1862 he returned to California as editor of San Francisco's *La Voz del Nuevo Mundo*. He returned to Los Angeles to run unsuccessfully for the state senate in 1863. He served as Los Angeles postmaster in 1864 and became state translator of California in 1865, both Republican patronage positions. Later he was connected with *La Crónica*, a Los Angeles newspaper launched in 1872, and practiced law in Los Angeles before settling in Ensenada, Baja California, in 1885. He was a successful lawyer and leading citizen there until his death in 1908.

Like many courageous journalists before and after him, Ramírez used the press to inform his readers of their rights, expose injustices and inspire action. His reports and editorials had a special ring of truth because he also was experiencing the same conditions he was reporting in his newspaper. He was not apart from what he was reporting, but was a part of what he was reporting.

Félix Gutiérrez is senior vice president and executive director of The Freedom Forum Pacific Coast Center in San Francisco. His family settled in Alta California in the early 1800s when it was claimed by Spain.

4

Ida B. Wells-Barnett

Journalism as a Weapon against Racial Bigotry

Pamela Newkirk

ON MAY 4, 1884, MORE THAN 70 years before Rosa Parks fueled the civil rights movement by refusing to give up her seat on a bus to a white man, 22-year-old Ida B. Wells spurned a segregated train car to sit in the ladies' coach. After she was forcefully removed from the coach, she exited the train, hired an attorney and sued the Chesapeake & Ohio Railroad Company on the grounds that blacks were relegated to the smoking car when the law called for separate and equal public accommodations. A court awarded her $500 in damages.

"Darky Damsel Gets Damages," reported the *Memphis Daily Appeal* on December 25, 1884. While the state supreme court reversed the circuit court ruling in 1887, the experience helped launch the career of a fearless journalist who unflinchingly put her livelihood and life on the line to confront racial injustice. After writing about her legal battle in a religious newsweekly, *Living Way*, Wells would for another four decades use journalism as a weapon against the virulent racial bigotry sweeping the South.

In 1889 Wells' *Living Way* columns under the pen name Iola were nationally circulated in black newspapers. That year she was invited to write for *Free Speech and Headlight*, which was co-owned by the pastor of Tennessee's largest Baptist church. Wells insisted on coming on board at *Free Speech and Headlight* as an equal partner. She became editor and one-third owner of the paper while maintaining her job as a Memphis public school teacher. For two years, she operated on dual fronts without incident. But in 1891, she turned her critical pen toward inferior conditions in the city's black public schools. The article cost her the coveted teaching job she had held for seven years.

She later wrote that she had tried to avoid losing her job by asking Rev. F. Nightingale, part owner and sales manager of the paper, to sign his name to the critical article. "I was still teaching and I wanted to hold my position," Wells wrote in her autobiography. When he refused, it was published unsigned, leading many to rightly assume she had written it.

Of her dismissal, she wrote, "Of course I had rather feared that might be the result; but I had taken a chance in the interest of the children of our race and had lost out. The worst part of the experience was the lack of appreciation shown by the parents. They simply couldn't understand why one would risk a good job, even for their children. ... But I thought it was right to strike a blow against a glaring evil and I did not regret it."

The loss of her job allowed Wells to turn her full attention to journalism. She was already known in black circles throughout the country as "Princess of the Press" for her contributions to many of the nation's leading black newspapers. The *New York Age*, the respected black weekly, regularly reprinted her Free Speech articles. Being an outspoken woman in a male-dominated profession only served to bolster her celebrity.

"She has become famous as one of the few women who handle a goose quill with diamond point as easily as any man in newspaper work," wrote T. Thomas Fortune, the legendary editor of the *New York Age*. "If Iola were a man she would be a humming independent in politics. She has plenty of nerve and is as sharp as a steel trap." Given the precarious status of blacks in the South during that era, when blacks were openly attacked by mobs, her outspokenness against the widespread disenfranchisement and persecution of blacks would have been noteworthy even for a man.

THIS WAS PARTICULARLY SO in 1892, when she began highlighting the widespread lynching of black men throughout the South, which had become a routine and publicly sanctioned form of justice. Her interest was piqued by the lynching of three prominent Memphis-area businessmen who managed a store in a heavily populated community. The men, Thomas Moss, Calvin McDowell and Henry Steward, had been charged, by a competing white grocery store owner, with conspiracy and indicted. The indictment triggered protests in Memphis' black community, and after four days of unrest, Moss, McDowell and Steward were charged with inciting a riot and thrown in jail. They were then taken from the county jail, shot and hanged, with graphic details of their lynching recounted in the daily newspaper. It was reported that Moss had begged for his life and that McDowell, whose fingers were shot off, had tried to grab the gun. For Wells, the incident both underscored the complicity of whites—in the government and in the press—in mob violence against blacks and debunked the prevailing myth that black men were lynched for raping white women.

In her editorial in Free Speech, Wells expressed outrage that "the city of Memphis has demonstrated that neither character nor standing avails the Negro if he dares to protect himself against the white man or become his rival." She implored blacks to "save our money and leave a town which will neither protect our lives and property, nor give us a fair trial in the courts, . . . when accused by white persons." She also urged blacks to continue a boycott of the streetcars in protest of the brutal murders.

She began to investigate the lynching of other black men accused of rape, including one reported in an Associated Press dispatch from Tunica County in Mississippi. "The big burly brute was lynched because he had raped the seven-year-old daughter of the sheriff," said the report. Wells set out for Tunica County, where she learned that the sheriff's daughter was a grown woman who had been found by her father in the black man's cabin. In another case, the victim's mother told her that her son had responded to the advances of the young mistress of the house and was lynched once their romance was discovered. Incidents such as these prompted her to write her now famous editorial published in Free Speech on May 21, 1892. In it, she questioned the purity of white women that was typically held up to justify the lynching of black men.

"Nobody in this section of the country believes the old thread-bare lie that Negro men rape white women," wrote Wells. "If Southern white men are not careful they will over-reach themselves and public sentiment will have a reaction; a conclusion will then be reached which will be very damaging to the moral reputation of their women."

The editorial sparked angry calls for revenge in the daily newspapers. "Patience under such circumstances is not a virtue," said the editorial in the *Evening Scimitar* of Memphis, Tennessee, on May 25, 1892. "If the negroes themselves do not apply the remedy without delay it will be the duty of those whom he has attacked to tie the wretch who utters these calumnies to a stake at the intersection of Main and Madison Sts., brand him in the forehead with a hot iron and perform upon him a surgical operation with a pair of tailor's shears." Given the male-dominated world of journalism at the time, the writer had little reason to suspect that the editorial had been written by a woman.

The same day, the city's *Daily Commercial* also called for revenge. "The fact that a black scoundrel is allowed to live and utter such loathsome and repulsive calumnies is a volume of evidence as to the wonderful patience of Southern whites. But we have had enough of it. There are some things that the Southern white will not tolerate, and the obscene intimations of the foregoing have brought the writer to the outermost limit of public patience. We hope we have said enough."

While Wells was en route to Philadelphia to attend the African Methodist Episcopal Church's general conference, the office of *Free Speech* was destroyed and its business manager, J.L. Fleming, was run out of town. Wells learned of the mob attack while meeting in New Jersey with Fortune, who showed her an account of the incident in the *New York Sun*. The article said that a group of leading citizens, acting on the *Commercial Appeal* editorial, had destroyed the type and furnishings in the Free Speech office and left a note warning that anyone who tried to publish the paper would be killed.

"Although I had been warned repeatedly by my own people that something would happen if I did not cease harping on the lynching of three months before, I had expected the happening to come when I was at home," Wells wrote in her autobiography. "I had bought a pistol the first thing after Tom Moss was lynched, because I expected some cowardly retaliation from the lynchers. I felt that one had better die fighting against injustice than to die like a dog or a rat in a trap."

URGED BY FRIENDS not to return to Memphis, Wells decided to stay in New York where she joined the staff of the New York Age. She was also given one-quarter interest in exchange for her *Free Speech* subscription list. "They had destroyed my paper, in which every dollar I had in the world was invested. They had made me an exile and threatened my life for hinting at the truth. I felt that I owed it to myself and my race to tell the whole truth," she would say later.

At the *Age,* Wells continued her aggressive crusade against lynching. She published a pamphlet, Southern Horrors: Lynch Law in All its Phases, which documented the epidemic throughout the South. It was the first time the atrocity against blacks had been thoroughly documented and the complicity of the white establishment highlighted. In many communities, white citizens would attend the public lynching of blacks—who were often set ablaze—for amusement. Such episodes were gleefully reported in the press. Wells was particularly horrified by a lynching in Paris, Texas, in February 1893 in which schoolchildren were given a holiday to see a murder suspect burned alive after being tortured for hours with red-hot irons.

"Brave woman! You have done your people and mine a service which can neither be weighed nor measured," wrote Frederick Douglass in a letter to Wells dated October 25, 1892, which she reprinted in her pamphlet on lynching, Southern Horrors. The documentation of lynching along with her national speaking tours in the United States drew international attention. She accepted an invitation to travel to England, Scotland and Wales in 1893 to publicize both the barbaric practice and the failure of prominent white Americans to condemn it. She riveted her European audiences with stories of American barbarity, and her speeches were widely reported on and editorialized. She was particularly critical of the American mainstream press, which was, at best, mute on the issue. "The pulpit and the press of our own country remains silent on these continued outrages and the voice of my race thus tortured and outraged is stifled or ignored wherever it is lifted in America in a demand for justice," she wrote in a letter to the editor published in the *Daily Post* in Birmingham, England, on May 16, 1893.

Wells' critique of the press earned her public enemies. The president of the Missouri Press Association, in a letter published in a local newspaper, denounced Wells and all black women who, he said, had "no sense of virtue and [were] altogether without character."

WHILE BEST KNOWN for her exposés on lynching, Wells wrote about a wide range of issues affecting African Americans. In 1893, in collaboration with Frederick Douglass, Ferdinand Barnett (whom she later married) and I. Garland Penn, they produced The Reason Why the

Colored American Is Not in the World's Columbian Exposition. The 81-page booklet condemned the exclusion of black Americans in the Chicago World's Fair. In the preface she wrote:

> The exhibit of the progress made by a race in 25 years of freedom as against 250 years of slavery would have been the greatest tribute to the greatness and progressiveness of American institutions which could have been shown to the world. The colored people of this great Republic number eight millions—more than one-tenth of the whole population of the United States. They were among the earliest settlers of the continent, landing at Jamestown, Virginia, in 1619 in a slave ship, before the Puritans, who landed at Plymouth in 1620. They have contributed a large share to American prosperity and civilization. The labor of one-half of this country has always been, and is still being done by them. . . . The wealth created by their industry has afforded to the white people of this country the leisure essential to their great progress in education, art, science, industry and invention.

In 1894 she returned to England, where for six months she lectured while regularly writing articles published in the newspaper the *Chicago Inter-Ocean.* She returned to the United States in July 1894. The following year she settled in Chicago and published A Red Record: Tabulated Statistics and Alleged Causes of Lynchings in the United States, 1892-1893-1894. She wrote:

> It becomes a painful duty of the Negro to reproduce a record which shows that a large portion of the American people avow anarchy, condone murder and defy the contempt of civilization. These pages are written in no spirit of vindictiveness, for all who give the subject [of lynching] consideration must concede that far too serious is the condition of that civilized government in which the spirit of unrestrained outlawry constantly increases in violence, and casts it blight over a continually growing area of territory. . . . During the year 1894, there were 132 persons executed in the United States by due form of law, while in the same year, 197 persons were put to death by mobs who gave the victims no opportunity to make a lawful defense. No comment need be made upon a condition of public sentiment responsible for such alarming results.

The *Red Record* provided not only statistics, most gathered through mainstream press accounts, but also a detailed overview of the history of lynching since the Emancipation Proclamation.

Wells married Ferdinand L. Barnett in 1895. Barnett, a lawyer, founded *The Conservator*, the first black newspaper in Chicago. The couple had three children, but Wells continued her newspaper work and anti-lynching crusade. She would later write for the nation's major black weeklies, most notably the *Chicago Defender*, for which she covered the race riots in Springfield, Illinois; Elaine, Arkansas; and East St. Louis, Illinois, the latter in which 150 blacks were killed in July of 1917. Her dispatches included interviews from scenes of violence, from the looted homes of blacks and from the municipal lodgings where blacks were driven by angry white mobs.

In the preface to her autobiography, Wells, who died in 1931 at the age of 68, maintained her fierce racial pride. She stressed the importance of blacks recording their own history, noting that the major accomplishments of blacks during Reconstruction—when blacks served in such high positions as lieutenant governor, governor and U.S. senator—were "buried in oblivion . . . [O]nly the southern white man's misrepresentations are in the public libraries and college textbooks of the land. The black men who made the history of that day were too modest to write of it, or did not realize the importance of the written word to their posterity."

It is something that could never be said of Wells-Barnett, who seemed always to realize the power—and the danger—of the written word.

Pamela Newkirk is an assistant professor of journalism at New York University and author of Within the Veil: Black Journalists, White Media.

5

Robert Capa and the
Spanish Civil War

Courage, Loyalty and Empathy

Richard Whelan

FROM 1936 TO 1954, ROBERT CAPA photographed five wars and set the standard by which photojournalists are judged. Of all the conflicts he covered, it was his first, the Spanish Civil War, that established his defining characteristics: passionate commitment, readiness to take sides, a willingness to share the hardships of the people he photographed and an ability to reconcile great ideals with sympathy and respect for individuals.

Growing up in Budapest, where he had been born Endre Friedmann in 1913 to middle-class Jewish parents, Capa (he took the more dramatic name in 1936) never dreamed of becoming a war photographer—or, indeed, a photographer at all. He was, however, interested in social and political reform. His mentor was poet and painter Lajos Kassák, who led a group dedicated to socialism and avant-garde art. Their magazine, *Munka* (Work), published the work of the American reformer photographers Jacob Riis and Lewis Hine.

As a teen-ager Capa planned on a career as a reporter. Journalism, he thought, would enable him to combine his loves of politics and literature.

As a result of his participation in leftist, pro-labor demonstrations against Adm. Miklós Horthy's conservative, anti-Semitic and authoritarian regime, Capa was exiled from Hungary in 1931, at the age of 17. He went to Berlin to study journalism, but the international economic depression soon forced him to leave school.

Through Hungarian friends he got a job as an errand boy and darkroom assistant at Dephot, a photographic agency that concentrated on human interest themes and represented an impressive list of photojournalists, where he was soon initiated into photojournalism. Dephot's founder, Simon Guttmann, an eccentric character active in German avant-garde art and radical politics, became one of the most influential in a succession of mentors for Capa.

Hitler's seizure of dictatorial powers after the Reichstag fire, late in February 1933, forced Capa to leave Germany. He first went to Vienna, where he stayed for a few months with the family of Dephot photographer Harald Leichenperg. He returned to Budapest briefly in the summer and then moved on to Paris.

In the spring of 1935, Capa's former boss at Dephot arranged for him to go to Spain to work on several assignments for German magazines. He went first to San Sebastián, where he did a story on the daily life of boxer Paolino Uzcudun, whose third fight with the German champion Max Schmeling was scheduled to take place in Berlin on July 7. Then Capa went on to Madrid to photograph Juan de la Cierva, who, in 1923, had invented a forerunner of the helicopter. Unfortunately he refused to show Capa his machine, saying that he was now interested only in linguistics.

Having covered the great parade in Madrid on April 14 to celebrate the fourth anniversary of the Spanish Republic, Capa proceeded to Seville for Holy Week. He felt a great affinity with the warmth, exuberance and generosity of the Spanish people, and his letters to his family, filled with accounts of his misadventures, read like a picaresque Spanish novel. With his dark good looks and his Spanish-sounding pseudonymous surname, Capa easily passed for a Spaniard—all the more so once he picked up a smattering of Spanish and began calling himself Roberto.

In July 1936 an alliance of monarchists and fascists, led by Gen. Francisco Franco, launched a civil war to overthrow the legitimately elected government of the Spanish Republic. Because Franco received aid from Germany and Italy, many young men and women in Europe and America felt that if they volunteered to aid the Republic, they would have an opportunity to fight fascism with more than words— and perhaps even to inflict a defeat so decisive that the international fascist movement would be universally discredited, thereby preventing the world war that otherwise seemed inevitable.

Both Capa and his girlfriend, the vivacious, clever and ambitious Gerda Taro, whom he had taught the rudiments of photography, were eager to use their cameras to win worldwide support for the Spanish Republic and the anti-fascist cause. They got their opportunity slightly more than two weeks after the outbreak of the war. Because Capa had recently had several very strong stories published in the French photographic magazine *Vu,* the owner of the magazine, Lucien Vogel, invited him and Taro to join a group of journalists he was flying to Barcelona to work on a special issue covering the Spanish Civil War.

After photographing in Barcelona, Capa and Taro went to the stalemated Aragón front, where they visited the militia of the Trotskyite POUM (Partido Obrero de Unificación Marxista) that George Orwell would serve with that winter. Capa and Taro then moved south toward Andalucía. Republican forces had begun an offensive to recover Córdoba, and the Madrid government reported new advances daily, even emptily boasting that its troops had entered the city. For photographers eager to cover Republican victories, the Córdoba front was a compelling destination.

There, just outside the tiny village of Cerro Muriano, on September 5, 1936, a 22-year-old Capa made one of his most famous images, perhaps the greatest of all war photographs—that of a Republican militiaman who has just been shot and is collapsing into death.

The internal evidence of the series of photographs to which that picture belongs suggests that Capa ran down a barren hillside with the vanguard of a Republican attack, and, as they came into range of an enemy emplacement, he threw himself down and hugged the ground (as we can see from the camera angle); from there he photographed several men as they were shot in succession. "Falling Soldier" received its first publication soon afterward in the September 23, 1936, issue of *Vu.*

In 1975, a controversy began over the authenticity of Capa's great photograph when O'Dowd Gallagher, an elderly British journalist of failing memory, charged that the photograph was staged. The claim was published in Phillip Knightley's book *The First Casualty: From the Crimea to Vietnam: The War Correspondent as Hero, Propagandist, and Myth Maker.*

In a world always eager to believe the worst, Gallagher's allegations spread rapidly. Refuting evidence was largely ignored. In September 1996, however, the controversy was definitively settled in Capa's favor by the discovery of the identity of the man in the photograph— Federico Borrell García, whose death at Cerro Muriano, on September 5, 1936, is recorded in the Spanish government's archives and whose identity in the photograph was confirmed by his younger brother, Everisto.

Through circumstantial evidence, which I pieced together while working on my biography of Capa, we know for certain that Capa and Taro were in Cerro Muriano on that day. Indeed, on the vintage prints preserved in the files of Capa's estate with their original chronological numbering, the numbers on the sequence of pictures to which the "Falling Soldier" belongs immediately precede those of a Cerro Muriano refugee series. The numbering on the vintage prints clearly suggested that Capa made his "Falling Soldier" picture at Cerro Muriano on September 5, 1936. Capa repeatedly confirmed during his lifetime that he had made his photograph on the Córdoba front.

OUT OF THE KIND of exploits that produced "Falling Soldier," Capa earned an enduring reputation for bravery. At a time when a photographer was lucky to get any credit line at all, the front page of the December 10, 1936, issue of the French weekly Regards acclaimed Capa as "Our special envoy to Madrid." Inside the editors said, "Regards, wanting to give its readers a faithful, irrefutable image of the tragic life of the inhabitants of Madrid, bombarded by the fascists, sent one of its most qualified and audacious photographers to the Spanish capital. . . . At peril of his life, he made a prodigious series of unique documents." Going even further, in December 1938 the prestigious British magazine *Picture Post* published 11 pages of Capa's Spanish Civil War photographs and proclaimed him "The Greatest War-Photographer in the World."

What inspired and sustained Capa when he went into the middle of battles—voluntarily and unarmed—to take photographs? First and foremost, he had the courage of his convictions. The Spanish Civil War was as much anti-fascist as it was Spanish, and that made it his war. He had a tremendous personal stake in its outcome, and he was willing

to die for the cause if necessary. Throughout his career Capa maintained that he was unwilling to risk his life covering any war in which
he did not love one side and hate the other. Moreover, he always felt
that it would be immoral to photograph men in combat without shar-
ing their risks and hardships. That attitude happened to serve his work
very well, for the trust and respect it won for him enabled him to get
more intimate and revealing pictures than he could ever have gotten
otherwise.

Capa's courage had several other bases as well. One, certainly, was
ambition. During his first two years in Paris, Capa had had little success in getting his work published. In the spring of 1936, he adopted
as his own the name Robert Capa—which he and Taro had originally
made up as the name of an alter ego, the imaginary character of a
glamorous and fabulously successful American photographer.

The young Hungarian was eager for success, and he understood that
the surest way to get it was to make pictures better than anyone else's.
But doing that was at least partly a matter of taking risks greater than
anyone else was willing to take. From the start, he worked in accor-
dance with what would become his most famous dictum: "If your
pictures aren't good enough, you're not close enough." Close enough
to the action, that is. (Of course, just being close to danger would
never guarantee good photographs. In Normandy he would write that
the most dangerous situations—such as mine fields—sometimes yield
the least exciting pictures.)

Capa also had the courage of the supreme confidence that comes
from winning the primal oedipal contest, from being the son whom the
mother loves above all other males in the family. He felt lucky and
blessed, as if he had a guardian angel protecting him. Unlike his friend
Ernest Hemingway, Capa never felt he had to prove his courage—to
himself or to anyone else. Indeed, Capa never boasted about his exploits. He was almost always the butt of his own stories, including one
about how he left his first major battle to change his pants, joking that
it was his first engagement and that his bowels had been weaker than
his feet.

In contrast to his insecure yet boastful friend Hemingway, Capa
was very much a gentleman of the old school—and gentle-men didn't
brag. Capa was also, like many others who are routinely exposed to
danger, rather superstitious. He believed that one shouldn't tempt fate
by bragging. Or by winning at poker. (He used to say that if he ever

started winning, that's when he would really get worried.) Translated into practical terms, Capa knew that being overconfident is the surest way to get killed in battle. In fact, the risks he took were carefully considered, never reckless. During World War II, generals Matthew Ridgway and James Gavin would praise Capa as a very shrewd judge of military danger.

Yᴇᴛ ꜰᴏʀ ᴀʟʟ ʜɪꜱ ꜰᴀᴍᴇ as a front-line photographer, Capa's pictures of Madrid during the Spanish Civil War make it clear that he was beginning to understand that the truth about war was to be found not only in the heat of battle, but also at the edge of things—in the faces of soldiers enduring cold, fatigue and tedium behind the lines and of civilians ravaged by fear, suffering and loss. Throughout his career, Capa was primarily a photographer of people. Many of his pictures of war are not so much chronicles of events as extraordinarily sympathetic and compassionate studies of people under extreme stress. He rarely photographed the dead or the grievously injured; instead, he focused on the survivors going on with life despite numbing losses and staggering destruction—the triumph of the indomitable human spirit.

In addition to his often-repeated advice about getting close to the action, he had another suggestion that was equally important and equally revealing: "Like people and let them know it." Whether Capa's photographs show soldiers or civilians, the pictures are characterized by intimacy and immediacy, by compassion and empathy. The horrific tendency of modern warfare is to depersonalize. Soldiers can use their terrible weapons of mass destruction only because they have learned to conceptualize their victims not as individuals but as a category—the enemy. Capa's strategy was to repersonalize the war—to emphasize that those who suffer the effects of war are individuals with whom the viewer of the photographs cannot help but identify. Confronted with overviews of a battle or of vast movements of refugees, one may feel simply overwhelmed and paralyzed. But the natural impulse of anyone who sees a photograph of an individual in pain or in need is to reach out and help.

Yet Capa, Gerda Taro and thousands of other anti-fascists from around the world could not save the Spanish Republic. Near the battle of Brunete in July 1937, Taro was mortally injured when a Loyalist tank sideswiped a car she was riding as she was standing on the running board. Capa, who was in Paris when he received the news, was overcome with grief. He traveled, covered Chinese resistance to the Japanese invasion in 1938, then returned to Spain to photograph the slow death of the Spanish Republic: the withdrawal of the International Brigades, the desperate attempts of Republican soldiers to defeat Franco's columns and finally the terrible plight of the refugees fleeing before the relentless Insurgent advance.

Capa went on to photograph the European theater of World War II (including the D-Day invasion), the first Arab-Israeli War and the war between French colonialists and the Vietminh in Indochina. The Indochina conflict, his fifth and final war, tested his belief that he was unwilling to risk his life covering a war in which he did not love one side and hate the other. Capa was by then the bearer of a United States passport but culturally French. As he rode through the countryside with a French convoy, he saw a French motorcyclist deliberately ride so close to the roadside that he forced some peasants to jump out of the way. Capa scornfully remarked to his colleague, *Time* correspondent John Mecklin, "Look at that s.o.b. making new Vietminh."

Later that day, while the stalled French traded fire with the Vietminh, Capa left the relative safety of the convoy to photograph troops advancing across a field. As he began to walk up the grassy slope of a dike, he stepped on a Vietminh anti-personnel mine. The explosion almost blew off his left leg and gave him a gaping chest wound. French troops rushed him to a Vietnamese doctor who pronounced him dead.

At a ceremony in Hanoi, a French honor guard stood by Capa's coffin. Draped over the casket was an American flag; pinned to it was one of France's highest military honors, the Croix de Guerre avec Palme, Order of the Army. More appropriate for Capa, who never cared much for military decorations, was a wreath from La Bonne Casserole, a Hanoi restaurant he frequented, inscribed simply, "A notre ami."

Capa's mother turned down the U.S. Army's offer of a plot in Arlington National Cemetery, saying that her son was not a soldier but a man of peace. At her request, a friend eventually arranged for Capa's burial in the cemetery of a Quaker meeting house.

Capa left behind an extraordinary body of work that showed war as it had never been shown before and displayed a tremendous sympathy for individuals in all kinds of circumstances. He also left a legend that would long continue to inspire other photographers and to delight and sadden his friends. In 1955, the Overseas Press Club and Life magazine created the Robert Capa Award for "superlative photography requiring exceptional courage and enterprise abroad." Among the recipients have been Horst Faas, W. Eugene Smith and Susan Meiselas. More than half a century after he ventured onto the battlefields of Spain, Capa still sets a standard of bravery and compassion for all war photographers.

Richard Whelan has written biographies of Robert Capa and Alfred Stieglitz. He is also author, with Evan Cornog, of Hats in the Ring: An Illustrated History of American Presidential Campaigns.

6

The Journalism of the French Resistance

An Underground War of Words

Pierre Albert

THE PERIOD AFTER THE GERMAN defeat of French forces in 1940, from the signing of the armistice on June 22, 1940, to the liberation of France in the summer of 1944, was a bleak time for the press. The Third Republic was terminated, and the country was divided in two. In the north and west, two-thirds of France was occupied by the German army, which held newspapers under its control with the help of collaborationist journalists. In the south, in Vichy, the government of Marshal Pétain also kept close watch on the press with its own censors: its editorial instructions left journalists little freedom of expression. After the Allies landed in North Africa, on November 11, 1942, the Germans invaded the so-called Unoccupied Zone governed by Vichy. From then on, newspapers were under the double dominion of Vichy and of the propaganda machine of the occupying forces.

By June 10, 1940, a majority of the 50 national dailies had stopped publishing. The others had followed the southward retreat of the French government and settled in cities such as Lyon, Clermont-Ferrand and Limoges. By the end of 1942, many of those that had moved south, like *Le Temps* or *Le Figaro,* decided to close shop so as not to function under the invaders' supervision. All the papers that continued to publish in France from 1940 to 1944 became, voluntarily or not, instruments of German or Vichy propaganda, serving "collaboration."

45

The only pluralist source of information the French then had was radio. Although the occupation forces and Pétain's authoritarian regime controlled their own stations, French people could, in spite of jamming, listen to "voices of freedom" from London, from French-speaking Switzerland, later from Algiers and also, from the United States, the Voice of America.

In this disastrous situation, journalists faced terrible dilemmas: if they refused to write, not only did they end their own careers but they made way for "collaborating" propaganda makers often recruited among the most despicable ranks of prewar journalism. If they continued to write, they submitted to the demands of the censors and to the orders of the occupiers—and thus cheated their readers. Only a few of the great journalistic pens took the way of exile in the summer of 1940 and went to Britain, such as Louis Levy of the daily *Le Populaire,* Georges Boris of *La Lumière* and Elie Joseph Bois of *Le Petit Parisien,* or went to the United States, like Pertinax of *L'Écho de Paris*, Pierre Lazareff of *Paris-Soir,* Émile Buré of *L'Ordre* and Geneviève Tabouis from *L'Œuvre.* In their host countries they worked for the Free French publications: *France, La France Libre, La Marseillaise* in London and *Pour la victoire* or *France-Amérique* in New York. French expatriates also published a large number of brochures and books.

TAKING AN INVENTORY OF underground publications is no easy task. Archivists and librarians find it hard to classify tracts, small posters, mere stickers and true periodicals whose names have often changed. The preserved collections of such material show gaps; moreover, it is often difficult to distinguish among local editions, which multiplied as early as 1941 and sometimes varied in their editorial contents. Overall, there were tens of thousands of tracts and more than 1,100 titles of periodicals—quite a few of them very short-lived.

The history of underground journalism nevertheless shows constant expansion. The first handbills appeared at the end of the summer of 1940: in the confusion and distress of the time, they expressed a refusal of defeat. Only a few copies of those simple tracts could be produced—handwritten, typewritten or reproduced by lithographic paste. Their anonymous, isolated authors recommended that readers copy them and thus widen the distribution. The use of stencil machines sometimes made it possible to make a few dozen copies. The first periodical to be printed was *Pantagruel,* whose first issue came out at the end of 1940. Its writer and editor Raymond Deiss, being a publisher of musical scores, owned an offset printer. He brought out 16 issues before he was arrested in October 1941. Two years later, he was beheaded in a prison in Cologne, Germany.

As early as 1941, periodicals began to multiply everywhere in France. With the complicity of small printers and of some typographers employed by the big authorized newspapers, the underground publications sometimes reached print runs of 5,000 to 10,000 copies. The format was kept small (usually the 21x27 cm format of sheet paper) and they ran only two to four pages (printed on one side only so they could be posted on walls) because paper was scarce. It was obtained from various sources, sometimes on the black market and sometimes by appropriating newsprint from the stocks of authorized publications.

The Resistance groups were scattered, and they devoted their first efforts at propaganda to creating underground publications. Very soon, they felt two further needs: federating their efforts and extending their action to other fields—intelligence gathering both for Allied and Free French services, infiltration of the Vichy bureaucracy, sabotage and, starting in 1943, the organization of paramilitary groups (maquis) and the preparation of the armed insurrection that would accompany the expected Allied landing. So it was around the publishers, printers and distributors of the underground press that the great Resistance movements were born at the end of 1942 and developed in 1943. They often took on the names of the major clandestine papers: *Combat, Défense de la France, Le Franc-Tireur, L'Insurgé, Résistance, Valmy, Libération Nord and Libération Sud.*

IN MAY 1943, A conseil national de la résistance (CNR) finally managed to gather all Resistance movements under its single authority, in allegiance to General de Gaulle's Free French. The underground press benefited a great deal from that consolidation. Its financial needs were largely covered by funds from the Free French: the money was indispensable as the clandestine newspapers were, of course, distributed free. The Resistance movements equipped themselves with genuine printing centers in large cities such as Lyon, Paris and Toulouse, which, besides printing newspapers, produced counterfeit identification documents—and even postage stamps—that were very useful to the underground. It was now possible for the better-managed titles to reach a circulation of more than 100,000 copies. Efficient distribution services sent out bundles of newspapers with the complicity of employees in the railroad and other transportation companies. Then the bundles were entrusted to volunteers who dropped the newspapers in letter boxes. Sometimes they were just flung around in university auditoriums or in the most populous streets.

In June 1942, a news agency was tentatively set up, the Bureau d'information et de presse, to be supplemented in April by a Comité d'information et de documentation: their bulletins were meant both for the publishers of underground sheets and for the Free French services in London. BBC and VOA broadcasts often consisted of quotes from those sheets. So did tracts scattered by Allied planes that made it possible for people in occupied France to discover a clandestine press many had never seen before. Conversely, exhibits of underground papers were organized in Britain, in South America and in the United States, which had some success at giving a concrete idea of the French people's fight against the occupying enemy.

At the end of 1943 and in the spring of 1944, the underground press experienced a boom. At that time, clandestine periodicals distributed nearly 1.5 million copies a month—in addition to hundreds of thousands of tracts. The higher circulations reached 200,000 to 250,000, including several regional editions. Those newspapers, usually monthlies, were supplemented by brochures of more than 50 pages like the Cahiers du Témoignage chrétien run by Pierre Chaillet, a Jesuit priest: 15 issues followed the first, with its epigraph "France, beware that you lose not your soul." From late 1941, the Editions de minuit (still alive in 2000) published two dozen real books, among which the very famous short novel *Le Silence de la mer* by Vercors in February 1942—the story of a francophile German officer facing the obdurate silence of the French family he was billeted to live with. The first print run of that book was 350 copies, but it was reprinted in Britain and widely distributed afterwards.

Those achievements came at a high price—ruthless repression by the Vichy and the German police. One of the first Resistance groups, that of the Musée de l'Homme, the great anthropology museum in Paris, published *Résistance*; it was shut down in February 1942 and seven of its members were executed—as were Jacques Decour, Jacques Salomon and Georges Politzer, who ran *L'Université libre*—in May 1942. Before Liberation in 1944, many other names were to be added to the list of press martyrs jailed, executed or sent to concentration camps from which few returned. As late as June 17, 1944, following a Gestapo raid in Villeurbanne, near Lyon, four typographers were shot dead in a villa harboring a printing press that produced regional editions of *Combat, Défense de la France* and *Le Franc-Tireur*. No particular statistics are available concerning those who worked for the underground press—but, taking the Défense de la France network as a whole, 688 of its 3,000 members were arrested, 127 executed and 322 sent to the camps, of whom 132 never returned.

Many stories bear witness to the determination of Resistance fighters and to their cunning. On Bastille Day 1943, Défense de la France (in its early days printed in the basement of the Sorbonne, then the major building of the University of Paris), organized an open distribution of its newspaper in metro trains, with its distributors protected by armed guards. In Lyon, on December 31, 1943, men from the Resistance went to street newsstands and replaced copies of the *Nouvelliste*, a collaborationist daily, with 25,000 copies of an imitation paper bearing the same name. The new *Nouvelliste* closely mimicked the original, down to its games, but presented a Resistance viewpoint. It was sold until the French police came, with no excessive haste, and seized the few remaining copies.

OVERALL, IN THE VAST and original operation that manufactured the underground press, press people played a minimal part. None of the major prewar barons of the French press took part in this new form of journalism. As for reporters and editors who were at work in the beginning of the war, quite a few entered the ranks of the Resistance—but not in a proportion any larger than for other professional groups.

The first publishers of underground sheets were journalists by chance. They were amateurs whose personal hostility to the Vichy regime motivated them to venture into journalism even though they were ignorant of its techniques. Actually, they operated as managers as much as writers: it was no big problem to fill the few pages of small size papers that came out at long intervals. And their political background varied. While the center of gravity in the Resistance was on the left, and a large part of the French right leaned toward fascism, underground press people (like their comrades in the larger Resistance) came from all political horizons, from the left and the right, and from all social classes. Political party militants, labor unionists, academics, members of the professions, students, writers, clergymen, lawyers and army officers switched to journalism—and were surprised to discover how easy it was to express their indignation and enthusiasm in short columns, or to comment upon events that they heard about on the radio or in the regular papers. Because most Resistance publications were monthlies, they did not cover daily developments in the war, which people could grasp by listening to the BBC every day. The underground press did, however, report on the local abuses by occupying forces and on local Resistance activities, which neither the collaborationist press nor the BBC would talk about.

The strict anonymity of the underground journalists and their use of pen names makes them difficult to study. And their more important activities had to do not with the writing but with printing and distribution—which involved the highest risk of arrest by the French or German police. Witness the following:

> Instructions by Combat in February 1942
> Let us recommend to you the utmost caution. Distribute the newspaper as fast as possible. Avoid keeping bundles of it at home for any length of time. Never send a package of papers by mail. Never write any name on a package or newspaper.
>
> Friendly readers, gather around us: set up small cells—we may one day have other things to ask of you. Last point, be discreet: do not try to know who makes your newspaper, do not try and find out where it comes from. . . . On the other hand, don't forget to have each copy read by a dozen of your friends. Let us not confuse caution and cowardice. Our newspaper is not meant for those who, comfortably ensconced in an armchair, would read it on the sly and then hasten to burn it for the sake of caution.

FROM 1943, THE FREE FRENCH authorities and l'Assemblée Consultative, a kind of parliament set up in Algiers—together with the CNR and the Fédération nationale de la presse clandestine, set up in occupied France in September 1943—carefully prepared the rebirth of a free press after the country was liberated. In the spring and summer of 1944, executive orders of the Provisional Government of the French Republic determined a press policy aimed at ending the corruption by business interests that had widely characterized the French press before World War II. It was quite smoothly implemented in the liberated regions and in Paris starting on August 24.

The French press then underwent a revolution vaster than that in any other European country. Every newspaper that had published for more than 15 days during German occupation, either after June 30, 1940, in the north zone, or after November 26 1942, in the south, was outlawed and its assets (buildings and equipment) sequestered and entrusted to the new press. The Provisional Government delivered licenses to publish to those newspapers that had stopped functioning before those dates, such as *Le Figaro, L'Epoque, Le Populaire, L'Humanité, L'Aube,* to the teams running underground papers and to a few new titles in parts of the country that had neither acceptable prewar papers nor any underground publications. All told, over 85 percent of the dailies in existence in 1940 thus disappeared. The purge severely struck the owners and journalists of the collaboration press: some were sentenced to death and about 10 were executed; others were jailed, and many were prohibited from working in the press again.

A few titles of the underground press survived the war. *Défense de la France*, born in 1941, published 47 clandestine issues and became *France Soir* in December 1944; that daily is still publishing in 2000, though considered moribund. *Le Franc-Tireur*, born in December 1941, tried hard to publish monthly, put out 37 issues, became *Paris-Jour* and died in the early '60s. *Combat*, born in December 1941, published 58 issues and survived until 1981. *Libération Sud*, born in July 1941, published 52 issues, became *Libération* (no link with the present daily of the same name), which was in the orbit of the Communist Party until the early '60s when the paper lost its Party subsidy and died. *Libération Nord*, born in October 1940, published 190 issues and then became Libé-soir, which died in the early '50s. *Ceux de la Libération,* born in May 1943, became *France Libre* and died in 1947. Le Populaire, born in July 1941, published 35 issues, was the daily of the Socialist Party until the late '50s. *Cahiers de l'O.C.M.* (Civilian and Military Organization) launched in June 1942, published four issues and became *Le Parisien libéré*, still one of the best-selling dailies in France. *L'Humanité,* the daily of the French Communist Party, was a special case. It went underground as early as the fall of 1939 because it had been banned by the French government after the German-Soviet non-aggression pact was signed. It became firmly anti-German only after Hitler decided to invade Russia in 1941. In all it published 316 issues.

New teams issuing from the Resistance, often endowed with more enthusiasm than experience, headed the new newspapers both in Paris and in the provinces. The papers enjoyed a very favorable status: founded without capital and without having had to invest in bricks and mortar or in manufacturing equipment, they also benefited from state subsidies on newsprint and on news (via the new wire service, Agence France-Presse) and for distribution. The Fédération nationale de la presse française stood watch over the material and moral interests of its members. The French were thirsty for uncensored information and critical comments, which they had missed during the dark years, so the prosperity of the newspaper market at the beginning of the Fourth Republic was guaranteed, at least at first. That new press started from scratch. Albert Camus, a journalist in Algiers and then for the underground *Combat*, became the editor of the new daily Combat. In an editorial of August 31, 1944, he very clearly expressed what had been the hopes of the members of the Resistance and what, he thought, was to be the new reality: a press controlled by journalists only:

> Our desire, all the more profound as it was often silent, was to liberate newspapers from money and to give them a tone and a veracity that would raise the public to the level of what is best in the country. We thought then that a country is as good as its press. And if it is true that newspapers are the voice of a nation, we were determined, insofar as our position and our modest capacity allowed, to raise the country by raising its language.

In the euphoria of recovered freedom, the sales of the 200 new dailies reached 15 million copies—far more than the 1939 circulation of 11.5 million. Actually, the expansion was artificial: the scarcity of newsprint restricted newspapers to four pages, often small size pages. By 1947, political and economic crises (food rationing lasted until 1949) caused many people to drop the overpoliticized papers. Competition became fierce. When the newsprint market returned to normal, the best-selling papers were able to increase the number of their pages and to siphon most of the slowly expanding advertising. In 1952, there were only 130 dailies left, and the total circulation had dropped to 9.5 million. Economic factors became dominant. In the Resistance, people had wanted to contain market forces by protecting the press from big business, but now it ruled again. Many of the titles born at the Liberation vanished. Camus and others had dreamed of a press entirely controlled by the journalists—but gradually the newspapers fell into the hands of publishers and managers.

Pierre Albert, professor emeritus of the Institut français de presse at the Université de Paris-2, is a leading historian of the French press. He is author of La France, les Etats-Unis et leurs presses *(1632-1976). This essay was translated by Claude-Jean Bertrand.*

7

This Female Crusading Scalawag

Hazel Brannon Smith, Justice and Mississippi

Bernard L. Stein

ON A HOT JUNE NIGHT IN 1963, Alfred Brown lay on the sidewalk in front of the honky-tonks on Yazoo Street in the small Mississippi farm town of Lexington, bleeding his life away. At a time when headlines and telecasts blazed with stories of confrontations between Southern blacks and police, his death went unremarked, except by the tiny weeklies responsible for keeping the residents of rural Holmes County abreast of the news.

"Alfred Brown, negro, was killed in an altercation with Lexington police on Yazoo Street Saturday night," reported the *Holmes County Herald* in a terse three-paragraph story. "Patrolman W. R. McNeer shot Brown in the chest as he advanced on him with a knife, Police Chief George Musselwhite said."

Author's note: "The way our people speak is part of our heritage and we're proud of it," explained the young students who compiled the marvelous oral history of the Holmes County civil rights movement, Minds Stayed on Freedom (Boulder, Colo.: Westview Press, 1991). I have followed their lead in not changing the way the people I interviewed speak. I have used courtesy titles, because it was clear from the way the people used them even when referring to close friends that they remain important to African Americans who were so recently denied this mark of respect. So important was being addressed as "Mr." or "Mrs." in Holmes County that the use of courtesy titles by merchants was one of three demands for ending a boycott of Lexington businesses in 1967.

Lexington's leading newspaper told the story quite differently. "Alfred Brown, a Negro Naval veteran of World War II and father of five children, was shot to death in Lexington Saturday night," the *Lexington Advertiser*'s story began.

The Advertiser's long and circumstantial account made it clear that the dead man, a mental patient who still wore the bracelet of the hospital from which he had just been released, was a victim of racist police. They pursued him down the street, accusing him of being drunk, shot him when he pulled out his pocket knife, then stood over him, guns drawn, to prevent his relatives and others who had gathered at the scene from going to his aid.

That the two stories appeared to arrive from different universes was no surprise. By 1963, the *Advertiser*'s editor and publisher Hazel Brannon Smith had become notorious, driving the racist powers that be of the region to flights of apoplexy. As state Rep. Wilburn Hooker of Holmes County told the director of the State Sovereignty Commission, the state agency established to spy on civil rights organizations, she was "this female crusading scalawag domiciled in our midst."

Holmes County, population 27,000, was desperately poor—but competing newspapers served it because Hazel Brannon Smith was a member of a small band of Southern journalists who supported the black movement for civil rights. The rival *Holmes County Herald* was founded by the segregationist white Citizens' Council in 1960 to drive her out of business. The Citizens' Council used the Herald to back up an advertising boycott of Mrs. Smith's two Holmes County weeklies, the *Advertiser* and the *Durant News*, which served the smaller city 12 miles east of Lexington.

Hazel Brannon Smith endured more than 20 years of violence, ostracism and economic strangulation in the name, she said, of "telling the people the truth and defending their freedom." In return for her suffering, she won the Pulitzer Prize for editorial writing in 1964, the first woman ever to be so honored. The usual burst of newspaper and magazine articles and speaking engagements followed the announcement of her Pulitzer Prize, and told the nation the story of the boycott of her newspapers, her husband's firing from his job as an administrator at the county hospital, the competition of the Citizens' Council paper, the Klan death threats and cross-burnings. Her enemies retaliated by bombing the *Northside Reporter*, her little weekly in Jackson that September. Three years later, just before the Advertiser was to go to press, arsonists set fire to the printing plant, causing major damage. The paper came out on time in a miniature edition printed on a small press sufficiently undamaged to be drafted into service. "When I am no longer free to print the truth unafraid, then you are no longer free to speak the truth without fear," the editor responded in her column. Ultimately, however, the campaign succeeded in driving Hazel Brannon Smith out of business—but not before her name became a symbol not just of courage, but of honor. Her nationwide fame has faded, her name is unfamiliar to a new generation of journalists, but her African American readers in Holmes County remember her vividly to this day.

HAZEL BRANNON SMITH did not set out to oppose Jim Crow. Three days after the Supreme Court proclaimed in 1954 that "segregated schools are not equal and cannot be made equal," Mrs. Smith attacked the decision in her column, "Through Hazel Eyes," a fixture on the front page of her eight-page newspapers. "We know that it is to the best interest of both races that segregation be maintained in theory and in fact—and that where it isn't maintained trouble results," she wrote. A month later, she added a hackneyed postscript: "Try as we may we cannot legislate human desires, appetites or emotions, prejudices and fears," and added, "we believe that intermarriage of the races is a sin—and that God did not intend for us to mix in marriage. If he had he would not have created separate races—only one."

Then, on the Fourth of July weekend, 1954, Sheriff Richard Byrd shot Henry Randall and Mrs. Smith's life began to change.

The sheriff, said the Advertiser, came upon a group of black men, started an argument with one, then pulled his gun and told him to "get goin.'" As the 27-year-old ran, the sheriff opened fire, wounding him in the leg. "Laws were made to protect the weak in our society from the strong," Mrs. Smith wrote in a signed, front-page editorial that called for the sheriff's resignation. "The vast majority of Holmes County people are not red necks who look with favor on the abuse of people because their skins are black." When Sheriff Byrd sued, she retorted, "Our defense against this alleged libel is the TRUTH," a defense an appellate court ratified, reversing a jury verdict that had found her guilty.

The memory of Mrs. Smith's refusal to look the other way when whites mistreated blacks remains strong in Holmes County's black community. James T. Wiley, now the mayor of Durant, who worked part-time in Mrs. Smith's print shop as a teenager, and whose late brother Will Edward Wiley was the mainstay of the printing operation, was among those who retold the story of the 1954 shooting in an interview in February 2000. "That didn't make her too popular," he said. "From that time on, things went downhill with her." From that time forward, as well, you will search in vain for a defense of segregation in the pages of the *Advertiser*.

Mrs. Smith's evolution from segregationist to active ally of the civil rights movement was gradual, however, until she agreed to print the *Mississippi Free Press,* a paper founded by activists to break the news blackout that had made it difficult to get word of their campaigns to black Mississippians. The newspaper greatly alarmed the Sovereignty Commission. On December 15, 1961, the commission's director and an investigator staked out the office of the Free Press in Jackson and saw Mrs. Smith and her husband speaking to Medgar Evers and members of the newspaper's staff. The investigators telephoned Rep. Hooker, touching off his "scalawag" outburst. Then they published their findings in an affidavit that the Citizens' Council mailed to legislators and the news media. State Sen. T. M. Williams, also from Holmes County, waved the affidavit on the senate floor as he denounced Mrs. Smith.

The editor struck back. Comparing the Citizens' Council to the Gestapo—an image that was to recur over the years—she said her papers had become the "chief target of a vicious statewide smear campaign." She sought to shift the terms of debate from civil rights to the First Amendment—and the use of taxpayer money to subvert it—by denying that the spies had observed a meeting. She was simply delivering a printing job, she insisted. Noting that both the Holmes County legislators who had attacked her were among the organizers of the rival *Holmes County Herald*, she traced their hostility to her refusal to suppress the story of Henry Randall's shooting. Somewhat disingenuously, for she must have known how controversial agreeing to print a civil rights newspaper would be, she claimed, "This battle is not an integration-segregation controversy at all."

MRS. SMITH COULD split hairs in this fashion because the revolt against Jim Crow had bypassed Holmes County. Although Sovereignty Commission spies were recording the license numbers of those attending NAACP meetings in the county as early as 1958, their few reports from the field were reassuring to segregationists. Sent to check on "subversive activities," in March 1961 a commission investigator reported that "everyone whom I talked to considered Hazel Smith, a white female, a trouble maker and integrationist," but added that civil rights activity was "at a low ebb."

That changed in the spring of 1963, when a group of black farmers journeyed to Greenwood to ask SNCC (the Student Nonviolent Coordinating Committee), the only civil rights organization brave, or foolhardy, enough to organize voter registration campaigns in Mississippi's backwoods, to help them found the Holmes County movement. Greenwood native John Ball immediately took up residence in the little black hamlet of Mileston to teach the farmers how to navigate the tortuous process of registering to vote. According to the U.S. Commission on Civil Rights, there were 4,773 white adults in Holmes County, and 4,800 registered white voters. Black adults numbered 8,757. Twenty were registered. So it was a momentous occasion when, on April 9, 1963, 14 black men, careful to walk into Lexington by twos so as not to appear to be demonstrating, approached the courthouse to register. A posse of 30 white men assembled by the sheriff greeted them, while a team of FBI observers watched. *The Advertiser's* story was low-key; by contrast, the *Herald* screamed of a "tense situation," as it reported that Deputy Sheriff Andrew Smith had formed the posse "as a precautionary measure should outsider agitators arrive and create trouble."

The first man to step across the threshold of the registrar's office that day was a farmer named Hartman Turnbow. A month later, night riders firebombed his home. The assailants chose Mr. Turnbow's little house near the railway tracks not only because of his audacity, but because John Ball had been sleeping in the back bedroom. They launched one of their Molotov cocktails through the bedroom window, but the organizer happened to be away. When Mr. Turnbow's wife and 16-year-old daughter fled from the flames, the night riders opened fire on them, but the farmer drove them off with his own rifle. The bombing brought John Ball back, along with three other SNCC workers, including Bob Moses, SNCC's top organizer in Mississippi, who was jailed at once when he tried to photograph the scene. The following day, Mr. Turnbow and the four civil rights workers were charged with setting the fire themselves.

While the *Herald* ignored the assault and later repeated the party line that the activists had faked the attack, Mrs. Smith was at pains to refute the claim. Three of the editorials in her Pulitzer Prize portfolio are concerned with the incident and the civil rights suit filed by the Justice Department that arose from it. She concluded the last with a warning to her white neighbors: "This is a world of change. The old ways of doing things will not suffice in this day and age. We cannot stop the clock. We ignore these facts at our own peril."

THE BLACK COMMUNITY reciprocated her support in many ways, few of which have been recognized in previous accounts of Hazel Brannon Smith's long ordeal. Individuals and the movement gave her their trust. "I mean she could talk to any black and whatever they know they warn't afraid to share it with her," recalled Walter Bruce, a civil rights activist. "And she come to a whole lot of meetin' that even some black folk was scared to come, but she'd always be at those meetin' and takin' notes and then the next week it's goin' to come out in the paper." As the Citizens' Council boycott tightened its grip on her advertisers, the income Mrs. Smith derived from job printing grew ever more important. When the storm broke over her printing of the *Mississippi Free Press*, Mrs. Smith told Jet magazine, "If every businessman in Holmes County doing business with Negroes should be deprived of that business, it would be only a short time until they were all broke." Asserting that printing the paper was just business may have been disingenuous, but the economic calculation contained a grain of truth.

"The only business that she could get, at least when I was working there, was from the black community," said Willie B. Davis, a retired high school science teacher, who worked his way through school at the print shop and who was particularly close to Mrs. Smith. The jobs were substantial. They included the monthly *Baptist Observer*, which Mrs. Smith edited as well as printed. Mr. Davis remembered sweating to get out books for the black Baptist Convention, the job he was working on when the printing plant was bombed in 1967. Reflecting on her evolution from the days when she supported segregation, he attributed the change to her reliance on African Americans for work in the plant as white advertisers deserted her papers. Not only did the boycott give her an economic incentive to support the aspirations of black people, he said, but also it brought her into increasing contact with them and deepened her understanding.

Another veteran of the *Advertiser* print shop, J. T. Wiley, who followed the example of so many Southern blacks and migrated north in search of economic opportunity, used his experience at the Advertiser plant to land a job as a printer at the *Defender*, Chicago's African-American newspaper. When Mrs. Smith spoke in Chicago in 1965, Mr. Wiley called to invite her to visit. Then he went to the *Defender*'s publisher and suggested that she write a series for the paper. "It helped her a while, you know, the money from that," he said.

A year and a half after winning the 1964 Pulitzer Prize for her "steadfast adherence to her editorial duty in the face of great pressure and opposition," Mrs. Smith was in such dire economic straits that supporters began fund-raising campaigns. *Columbia Journalism Review* launched a nationwide appeal to members of the profession. It yielded not quite $2,700. But just before Thanksgiving, the poor black farmers, teachers, preachers and businesspeople of Holmes County filled the auditorium at Saints Junior College in Lexington to overflowing for Editor's Appreciation Day, where the college president presented Mrs. Smith with a handmade box decorated by teachers. Inside it was an orchid and $2,855.22.

"Of all the people in the world, I think I am the most blessed," wrote the beleaguered editor in the next edition of the *Advertiser*. "It was the most wonderful day of my life."

Shortly thereafter, the organizers of Editor's Appreciation Day formed a support committee to serve as a permanent counterweight to the Citizens' Council boycott. In 1965, the Holmes County civil rights movement flexed its muscles with demonstrations, a renewed voter registration campaign and a push to integrate the schools. In September, an anonymous two-page tract threatened retaliation and singled out Mrs. Smith, warning, "Her Communist financed holiday in Holmes County is just about over." Odell Durham, whose children were among the first African Americans to attend Durant's previously all-white elementary school that fall, still remembers how vulnerable she felt when she opened her front door to find that leaflet, left on her doorstep during the night. Thirty-five years later she can still quote its concluding threat almost word for word. The civil rights movement responded with a selective buying campaign directed at local business. An unnamed "prominent Negro" told the *Advertiser* the campaign was sparked by deep resentment of the school boycott and by "the way they have treated Miss Hazel." Two years later, the movement made its support for Mrs. Smith explicit. Among the three objectives of a new selective buying campaign was a demand that the city, county and local businesses advertise in her papers.

AS HER FAME SPREAD, Mrs. Smith was at pains to portray herself as a moderate, perhaps in an effort to appeal to as broad a base of support as she could. "I don't approve of enforced integration any more than enforced segregation, but there ought to be a middle ground," she told Sue Ann Wood of the *St. Louis Globe-Democrat* after winning the Golden Quill Award of the International Society of Weekly Newspaper Editors in 1963. When the National Council of Women named her the "Woman of Conscience" for 1964, she told the audience at the Biltmore Hotel in New York that she did not want to be characterized as "a crusading newspaper editor." Her friend Hodding Carter also influenced the way journalists and scholars portrayed her. "Nowhere outside the Deep South would Hazel Brannon Smith be labeled even a liberal in her racial views," he asserted in an article published in the *St. Louis Post-Dispatch* in 1961, reprinted in his book *First Person Rural* in 1963. "If she must be categorized, then call her a moderate." Thirty years later, the academic historians Neil McMillen, Charles M. Payne and John Dittmer followed suit.

None of them can have read and absorbed the body of Hazel Brannon Smith's writing during the civil rights era. From the time the Holmes County movement began with the arrival of SNCC organizers in Mileston and Hartman Turnbow's effort to register to vote in 1963, relentlessly, week in and week out, "Through Hazel Eyes" and her editorials advocate justice for African Americans. They burn with indignation. Not once during those years did Mrs. Smith call for compromise. Not once did she suggest that a demonstration be called off. Not once did she conclude that the freedom movement was moving too fast or too far. She did not criticize the movement's tactics, even when they included economic pressure, although she had often said it was the Citizens' Council's use of boycotts that originally led her to oppose the organization. While most of Mississippi's journalists joined its politicians in denouncing "outside agitators," Mrs. Smith welcomed the 33 Freedom Summer volunteers who came to Holmes County to organize Freedom Schools and register blacks to vote. "One of the most popular misconceptions in Mississippi is the idea that if everyone would just leave us alone we would work out all our problems and everything would be fine. . . . The truth is we have been left pretty much alone for nearly one hundred years—and we have not faced up to our problems as well as we should," she wrote.

As schools opened in September 1965, the one-time segregationist pressed white families to abandon their boycott of integrated classes and return their children to the public schools. "Mississippi has no future without a strong public school system. Neither does Holmes County," she declared in a front-page editorial. While she summoned her greatest passion to assail attacks against African Americans and threats to her newspapers, she did not advocate nonviolence, reporting matter of factly when black farmers established armed brigades to protect homes and meeting places threatened by night riders. When she got a threatening phone call in February 1966, she minced no words concerning her attitude toward self-defense. "The first one that put his foot on my home grounds would have been shot dead," she wrote in "Through Hazel Eyes." "The same goes for any future intruders—stay away from my home if you don't want to get killed. And you may consider this a public notice and fair warning." Mrs. Smith came to understand how obdurate and how powerful the opponents of equality were. Writing about the assassination of Martin Luther King, whom she called "a modern messiah," she lamented that "there has been little change in the white man's mind and virtually no change in the white man's power structure. Every step forward has had to be forced—with the ballot, the boycott and continuing tensions and pressures." The editorial ended on a pessimistic note: "We hold our future in our own hands—but we are by no means certain white America will be worthy or equal to the task of preserving this beloved nation."

Hazel Brannon Smith was no moderate. She was a wholehearted supporter of integration and of black political power who loathed the intertwined apparatus of the government, Citizens' Council and Klan that underpinned American apartheid.

IN THE END, the sympathy and indignation her plight aroused could not save Hazel Brannon Smith. The roof literally fell in on her printing press. Impoverished and beginning to show signs of Alzheimer's disease, in 1985 she closed the second oldest newspaper in the state and moved in with her sister's family, to the home she had grown up in in Gadsden, Alabama. She died, nearly destitute, in a nursing home in Tennessee in 1994. To this day, the derelict *Advertiser* building in the shadow of Lexington's town square sits open to the elements, as though to remind those with long-enough memories of the price of defiance.

Did her passion and her sacrifice make a difference? That's not an easy question to answer. Over and over again she asserted that most white people in Mississippi were decent and could be aroused from their torpor if she could help them overcome their fear. "Surely one day, some of my former friends will come to understand it is their personal freedom for which I have been fighting as well as my own," she wrote plaintively in 1966. If they did, they kept quiet about it.

Most of the courage and all of the effort to achieve racial justice came from Holmes County's African Americans. They built the Freedom Democratic Party, which continues to meet on the third Sunday of each month to this day. They elected the state's first black representative since Reconstruction. In 124 lawsuits they sought school integration and voting rights and challenged discrimination. They marched and picketed and boycotted businesses and on more than one occasion engaged in gun battles with night riders. Yet Mrs. Smith is remembered in Holmes County's black community. A group of men passing the time this February in a small convenience store, near the spot where Alfred Brown fell, talked of the killing and of Mrs. Smith's exposé as though it had happened four days, not four decades, ago. Her unflinching reporting of assaults on black residents was a recurring theme in interviews with participants in Holmes County's civil rights movement and with African Americans who had worked for her. Her newspapers "let the peoples know what was going on and didn't hide anything," said Odell Durham, who joined the movement in 1964 when a white Freedom Summer volunteer knocked on her door and asked, "Don't you want equal rights?" Even before he met her, recalled Willie B. Davis, who worked at the Advertiser printing plant in the 1960s, he knew "if anyone was doing anything to blacks in Holmes County, Miss Hazel was going to write it. She's going to expose them." Walter Bruce explained that participants in the movement trusted Mrs. Smith because "well, you know like somebody getting beat up or something—they tried a pretend it happened thisaway and she just outspoken, and whatever she believed in, you know, this is what happened, that's what she put in her paper." Mayor Wiley concurred: "She'd write an editorial, you know, she wrote what she believed happened, and that just wasn't a popular thing at that time."

Today in Holmes County, as in other Mississippi counties where African Americans form the majority, blacks are well represented in the ranks of politicians, police officers and government workers. But although the movement swept away legal segregation, the public schools of the county are virtually all black. White children attend private academies. On a driving tour of Lexington, Mr. Davis pointed to a new development of luxury homes. "A lot of black folks don't even know these streets exist," he said. Elsewhere, he identified streets as black or white, with just a few housing people of both races. The very poorest homes—sagging little shotgun shacks—house black families.

"It has been a big difference, but it's still a whole lot of work to do. Goin' always be marchin.' One hundred thousand years from now goin' to still be marchin,'" Mrs. Durham summed up.

All the African Americans I interviewed believe the bloody record of repression in Holmes County would have been still worse without Hazel Brannon Smith. "Can you imagine Lexington without the *Lexington Advertiser*? Or Holmes County without Hazel Brannon Smith? Why they would put your eyes out," said Dr. Arenia Mallory on Editor's Appreciation Day in 1965. "Had it not been for her paper, the abuse that was happening I think it would have been on a larger scale. It was somewhat curbed because of the fact that they knew that Hazel would print it—regardless, she would print it," said Mr. Davis. Several movement veterans also found in Mrs. Smith's story some reason for optimism, because a white person showed the capacity to change and the willingness to join with them. "I think she helped people to believe that we can achieve a semblance of justice," said LaVerne Lindsey, a plaintiff in a groundbreaking discrimination suit against the Mississippi Cooperative Extension. Hazel Brannon Smith was part of the movement, said Mr. Bruce. "I don't really think she could have put no more in than she did."

Bernard L. Stein, a winner of the Pulitzer Prize for editorial writing, has been editor of The Riverdale Press, *the Bronx, New York, weekly founded by his father, since 1978.*

8

L. Alex Wilson

A Reporter Who Refused to Run

Hank Klibanoff

THE SIDEWALKS AND STREETS surrounding the massive Central High School in Little Rock had become forbidding for blacks and foreboding for reporters in the edgy three weeks after Arkansas Gov. Orval Faubus abruptly derailed school desegregation in September 1957.

Confident that the Negroes would be kept out by the cordon of Arkansas National Guardsmen surrounding the school, crowds of angry whites—many having no connection to the school or to Little Rock—arrived every morning to demonstrate their disapproval of integration. They watched white students enter the school and kept a watchful eye to make sure black students, though backed by a federal court order allowing them in, didn't try to sneak in. White reporters and cameramen faced relentless heckling, physical taunts and spittle. Black reporters faced worse. The story had drawn many of the most experienced journalists in the black press, reporters who had braved the back roads of the South and pioneered civil rights coverage long before it caught on with the mainstream white press. But as they tried to penetrate the scene around the high school, they met scorn and stonewalling as National Guardsmen quickly moved them off the premises and away from the story.

On the warm Monday morning of Sept. 23, the integration stalemate broke and the story changed. The National Guard, following a federal court edict, had withdrawn. The white crowds stayed, however, leaving the school's grounds and perimeter beyond the control of authorities. Black students on their way to the school in a station wagon were heading into an unpredictable mob scene.

At the same time, in a separate car, intent on witnessing and covering the moment firsthand, were four seasoned black newsmen. Their leader was the tall, dark-skinned and serious L. Alex Wilson, the editor and general manager of the Tri-State Defender of Memphis, Tennessee—the newspaper that was the southern outpost of the *Chicago Defender*, one of the foremost black newspapers in the United States.

Wilson, the most honored of the black journalists on the story and, at age 49, the senior member of the group, was behind the wheel. He was accompanied by Jimmy Hicks, editor of the *Amsterdam News* of New York City, Moses Newson, formerly of the *Tri-State Defender* and now on his first assignment for the *Baltimore Afro-American*, and Earl Davy, a commercial photographer carrying a Graflex camera who was taking pictures that day for the local black newspaper, L.C. and Daisy Bates' *Arkansas State Press*.

Wilson parked the car and led the way as the four newsmen started walking toward the school. His height, 6-foot-4, and darkness made it impossible for him to enter the scene unnoticed. He carried himself with dignity but without a hint of haughtiness. As tall as he was, he was not imposing. His shoulders were somewhat sloped and he carried himself slightly bent forward, in the manner not of a black man trying to make himself less intimidating to a white world, but of a tall man trying to negotiate a world of shorter people.

Wilson was dressed smartly, but not flamboyantly, in a dark, crisp suit. He kept his coat fastened at the middle button and wore a tan, wide-brimmed hat. As Wilson and the other newsmen walked, he could see they were approaching a crowd of white people that numbered in the hundreds and was growing, it seemed, with each step forward. Within moments, he could feel the angry presence of white men gathering behind him and gaining ground.

"Get out of here!"

"Go home, you son of a bitch nigger."

Two men jumped in front of the newsmen and spread out their arms. "You'll not pass," one said.

"We are newspapermen," Wilson responded.

"We only want to do our jobs," said Hicks.

"You'll not pass."

With anger and chaos seething all around him, with racist hatred running wildly out of control and with the possibility that he and his colleagues would die on the streets of Little Rock, Wilson would come face-to-face with a vow he had silently made to himself many years earlier: He would not, under any circumstances, show fear or run. The day would be as fateful for Wilson as it was for the nine Little Rock students and for the nation.

CIVIL RIGHTS WAS a series of disparate events not yet called a movement, and the honor roll of modern civil rights martyrs was still short, when John H. Sengstacke, the *Chicago Defender* publisher and editor, looked south in 1951 and saw opportunity.

In Memphis, pivotally positioned to cover Tennessee, Mississippi, Arkansas and Alabama, Sengstacke saw a chance to gain a foothold with a black-owned, black-focused weekly newspaper that could cover the frontier of the emerging civil rights story more quickly, more aggressively and with greater impact than could his Chicago staff.

Success was not certain. Sengstacke would be going head-to-head with an equally prominent black newspaper family, the Scotts of Atlanta, whose World newspapers in Atlanta, Birmingham and Memphis were well established and traditional reading in black households in the South. The *Memphis World*, for example, had been publishing for two decades. The Scotts reflected the politics of the prewar black South: while they demanded the full rights of citizenship for all black Americans, they were gradualists. They were outspoken against agitation that went beyond their editorial pages, and they tended to give the white establishment the benefit of the doubt.

As the 1950s began, much of the black press was already onto stories of brutality that the white press was missing, ignoring or belittling. Few black leaders died as heroes in the white press, North or South. In much of the Southern white press, early leaders who were killed for their activism were portrayed as dying in freakish incidents or under mysterious circumstances or of self-inflicted wounds. It would be the black press that would seek and discover evidence of homicide where sheriffs found none. The 1955 death of Rev. George Lee, a pastor of four churches, a grocer and a leader of a voter registration drive in the Mississippi Delta, was treated as an "odd accident" in the

Jackson, Mississippi, *Clarion Ledger*, leaving it to the black press to point out that his pierced vocal chords and the lead pellets embedded in the remains of his face suggested homicide. Similar differences in coverage came that year after the murders of Lamar Smith in Brookhaven, Mississippi, and Clinton Melton in Sumner, Mississippi.

But getting to the stories was difficult. The black press typically didn't fly to assignments, and bus rides into the backwaters were fraught with danger and, of necessity, cloaked with deception. Black reporters dispatched from Pittsburgh, Baltimore, Chicago and Detroit to cover stories of lynchings, beatings and castrations would shed their suits and ties and put on dusty bib overalls and a low-headed shuffle in order to slip into a Southern town and start reporting.

To Sengstacke, the closer he could get his reporters to the action, the better. To raise the flag over his new paper and send the message that it was ready to take on the South, Sengstacke in 1952 sent one of his most trusted reporters and editors to Memphis to serve as general manager and to rally the newspaper—L. Alex Wilson.

Sengstacke got more than a good Memphis paper out of the deal. He got a newspaper perfectly positioned in time and geography to cover the dawn of the civil rights activities in the region, "as if cued to appear by some divine plan," Wilson's wife, Emogene, herself a newspaperwoman, would write later.

WILSON, BORN IN Orlando, Florida, in 1908, had known as a child that he wanted to be a newspaperman. Most afternoons, he would come home from school and disappear into his bedroom, where his mother would find him writing, writing, writing. He got his bachelor's degree at Florida A&M, studied in the highly regarded journalism program at Lincoln University in Missouri and did graduate work at the University of Wisconsin and Roosevelt College in Chicago before serving as a Marine in World War II.

Wilson turned first to teaching, becoming an assistant principal, then principal, of high schools in north central Florida. In racial temperament, north central Florida was historically only slightly less virulent than the worst parts of the South.

In the same way that Emmett Till would become the most defining event in the childhood lives of Negro children in Mississippi, the terrifying story of Claude Neal made an indelible impression on Negro residents in north and central Florida. Neal, accused in 1934 of killing a white woman, had been dragged by a mob from an Alabama jail. As Neal was being transported to Marianna, in the Florida panhandle, newspaper and radio stories gave advance notice of the lynching, giving about 4,000 people time to get to the scene. Neal was scalded repeatedly with a hot iron, castrated and dragged through the streets before being stretched and displayed in a tree. By some accounts, he was forced to eat his own genitals, and his fingers and toes were put on display in the town.

In Leesburg, Florida, where Wilson was teaching, the Ku Klux Klan periodically paraded through town to intimidate Negro residents, who needed little prompting to conjure the image of Claude Neal and other victims. The first time Wilson saw such a parade, he had an epiphany that would influence his behavior on the streets of Little Rock. As the Klan muscled its way through town, Negro residents scattered in fear. Wilson was among them. Forever after, Wilson hated himself for fleeing. He never forgot it, he never forgave himself, and he vowed never to run away again.

From teaching, Wilson turned to journalism to fulfill his childhood ambition to write, working for a number of newspapers before landing at the influential *Norfolk Journal and Guide* in Virginia. He won a reputation as a terrific reporter. As a correspondent covering the Korean War, he won black journalism's highest honor, the Wendell Wilkie Award. His demeanor underscored that reputation. His clipped, professorial speech and his stern visage provoked uprightness and formality in others, so much that his colleagues—even in their most casual, shorthand conversations—frequently referred to him not as "Alex" or "Wilson" but as "L. Alex Wilson." He could be so dour, his friends joked, that he didn't smile much because it hurt when he did.

Still, Wilson's colleagues marveled at his ability to work his way inside fortresses of white power and come out with something without seeming to compromise anything. Soon after signing up with Sengstacke and arriving in Memphis, Wilson moved quickly to establish the *Tri-State Defender* as authoritative, essential reading for anyone interested in politics there.

In 1955, Wilson's eloquent editorial support for mayoral candidate Edmund Orgill helped produce a record black turnout on Election Day and an Orgill victory. That same year, Wilson editorially censured the Peabody Hotel for allowing blacks only limited use of the hotel under demeaning conditions. Two years later, Wilson's news and editorial pages strongly supported a boycott against the Memphis Commercial Appeal until it finally agreed to make significant changes in its coverage of blacks, including use of the same courtesy titles accorded whites mentioned in stories.

Under Wilson, the *Tri-State Defender* relentlessly pursued equal opportunity and maintained a healthy sense of outrage. When members of a U.S. Senate subcommittee asked Nobel Peace Prize-winner Ralph Bunche if he was a Communist, the *Defender* warned, "The Statue of Liberty will be next."

In the fall of 1955, when word leaked out of the Delta that Emmett Till—a black, 14-year old Chicago boy—had been carried off from his uncle's home at night by two white men, no newspaper, black or white, was better prepared than the *Tri-State Defender*. Even before Till's naked, tortured, bloated and decomposing body emerged from the Tallahatchie River three days after he was abducted, Wilson was working the story with another *Tri-State Defender* reporter, Moses Newson, a fellow Floridian and Lincoln University journalism alum with whom he would walk the mean streets of Little Rock two years later, and with black photographer Ernest C. Withers. Over the next several weeks, their stories and photos, topped by giant, boldface headlines, would dominate the *Defender* papers in Chicago and Memphis.

The Till trial took place in Sumner, Mississippi, only three weeks after the abduction. From the first day, black reporters were subjected to a sheriff whose daily courtroom greeting was " 'Mawning, nigguhs." Following an appeal by Wilson and some white reporters, including *The New York Times'* Johnny Popham, the judge intervened with the sheriff and had a large table set up in the courtroom for about 10 black reporters and photographers.

Even the harshest critics of Jim Crow justice believed that the prosecutor was making an earnest effort to convict the defendants and that the judge was being fair-minded in his handling of the case. But the sheriff's investigation was lackadaisical, and the prosecutor lacked witnesses that everyone in the black community knew existed: the field hands who had seen Till with the defendants in their truck, who had seen the truck drive into a barn, who had heard the beating and screaming, and who had seen the truck leave the barn and head for the river. Indeed, word was out that two of the field hands had been on the truck with Till, had been inside the barn during the beating and had been ordered to clean the blood from the barn floor.

Encouraged by prominent black leaders in the Delta, Wilson and a group of enterprising black journalists decided to seek out the witnesses themselves. A couple of white reporters were brought in to the hunt as well; their credibility with white law enforcement authorities would be needed in order to hand over the witnesses. Working deep into the night as the trial was in progress, Wilson and the others drove bravely across the dirt roads that spiderwebbed through the flat cotton fields and led to the doors of sharecropper homes. Eventually, the reporters pulled in three witnesses who reluctantly agreed to testify and who lent great weight to the prosecution's case. But the two who were said to have been inside the barn eluded the searchers.

The jury took an hour to acquit the defendants. "If we hadn't stopped to drink pop," said one juror, "it wouldn't have taken that long." The verdict was not unexpected but upset Wilson nonetheless. He decided to stay on the case, to drive deeper into the Delta seeking the other witnesses. "The smooth hum of the auto motor did not dispel the danger involved in the mission," he later wrote in the Defender papers. "I was not shaken by fear. I had decided before leaving home, and after communing with God, that if I could in any way help to contribute anything to justice in this shameful case ... whatever the price, so be it." After four days that he described as "harrowing, danger filled," Wilson finally tracked down one of the supposed witnesses, Levy "Too Tight" Collins, and drove him to Chicago to be questioned for two days by the newspaper's general counsel.

For days, the Chicago and Memphis papers made an enormous splash with Wilson's coup and featured front-page photographs showing "Too Tight" sitting with Sengstacke. In the end, Collins denied knowing anything about the murder. Wilson's articles made it clear he didn't believe Collins: "Collins' denial does not completely clear him of implication in our knowledge of the crime," Wilson reported. "There remains a haunting suspicion that Collins knows more than the *Defender* was able to elicit from him."

TWO YEARS LATER, trying to get into position to chronicle history on the streets of Little Rock, Wilson was facing an even more harrowing, danger-filled encounter. Feeling the heat of angry white men blocking him and his three colleagues from front and behind, Wilson turned to a policeman and showed his press card. "You better leave," the policeman said. "Go on across the sidewalk." Wilson and the others obeyed, only to realize that the officer had let the white thugs follow them and close in. "Anyone got a rope?" one white man shouted. "We'll hang 'em. I can get one awful quick."

In a phone booth nearby, Associated Press's top spot reporter, Relman (Pat) Morin, was just finishing a conversation with Little Rock bureau chief Keith Fuller. "Not much to report," Morin told Fuller. He dictated some color and was wrapping it up when he heard the piercing yell of whites who saw Wilson, the photographer Earl Davy and the two other newsmen, Jimmy Hicks and Moses Newson, heading their way: "The niggers are coming!"

Morin saw everyone turn away from the school and move in a new direction. "Hang on!" Morin yelled into the phone, "Hang on! There's a helluva fight starting."

"Roll it," Fuller told Morin calmly. Turning quickly to another editor at the office, Fuller blurted, "Get ready for a bulletin."

Suddenly, two men, one wearing a crash helmet, assaulted Davy. They caught him, muscled him toward some high grass and slugged and kicked him. Others smashed his Graflex camera onto a concrete sidewalk, destroying his film. Another group of white men sputtered curses as they kicked and hit Newson and Hicks until the reporters broke free and ran away.

Morin, with a clear view inside the phone booth, held his position, opened the door to hear the commotion better and breathlessly dictated everything he saw and heard.

As the assault continued, the station wagon with the nine black students eased up to the south entrance of the school, and the students and two adults emerged. As they entered Central High, they examined the crowd with curiosity but little interest.

Meanwhile Wilson—taunted, pushed and slapped as he kept walking—was suddenly rushed from behind by a man who planted one foot, swung the other as hard as he could in the manner of a field goal kicker and slammed his shoe into the base of Wilson's spine. Another man kicked Wilson so hard that the reporter's lanky frame looked as if it would fold. Still, he lurched forward. Seeing that his hat had been knocked to the ground, Wilson stopped. Slowly, almost casually, as if to give them no credit for altering his course, he bent down to pick it up. In that moment, he had a chance to run, and he might well have been able to get away. But he had made that vow, long before, in Florida. "I decided not to run," he wrote later. "If I were to be beaten,

I'd take it walking if I could—not running."

As the mob darted in and out at him, throwing punches and kicks, Wilson picked up his hat, stood erect and took some time to run his hand along the crease. His refusal to show fear infuriated the mob. "Run, damn you, run," one man yelled. More punches came. Wilson, though surrounded, moved ahead.

As television cameramen and still photographers recorded the action, a man jumped onto Wilson's back and wrapped his left arm around Wilson's neck in a stranglehold. Two feet away, a burly man gripping a brick stared at the immobilized Wilson, ready to start swinging. But he couldn't. A man standing beside him kept a tight grip on his arm, preventing him from swinging the brick. As the man on Wilson's back drove him to the ground, the man with the brick got close enough to crack Wilson's skull. Again he was pulled back. Finally the man with the brick settled for a hard kick into the center of Wilson's chest. Wilson, hiding his anger, looked at the man and wished at that moment that he could meet him one-on-one.

Wilson, still holding his hat even as he fell to the ground, raised himself up, recreased his hat and kept walking. He looked straight ahead. Then he took one last powerful blow to the head—some witnesses later said it was the brick this time—before being pushed away by the crowd. The nine Negro students had quietly slipped into the high school.

As the mob went wild with the realization that the school had been integrated, Wilson walked to his car. He still had not unfastened the middle button of his suit coat.

Wilson was hurt in two ways that day. When he dictated his story, he noted that the attack on the journalists served as a decoy while the nine students entered Central High School. The story's headline in the *Tri-State Defender* said the journalists participated in a ruse to help the students. Wilson had not meant to suggest that the decoy was purposeful; it had just turned out that way as the attack coincided with the arrival of the students.

Wilson was able to correct that misimpression in the next issue. What he couldn't correct—what he didn't even recognize initially—was the permanent physical damage he sustained that day.

Wilson's performance in Memphis earned him a promotion, to become editor of the larger and more influential *Chicago Defender*. Not long after he arrived in early 1959, he began experiencing what his wife called a "nervous ailment," which seems likely to have been Parkinson's Disease. As his situation worsened, Wilson's wife and friends concluded that the condition had been brought on by the beating he took in Little Rock.

Wilson died on Oct. 11, 1960, at age 51. His body was returned to Memphis for burial. *The Tri-State Defender* ran a photograph across the top of its front page showing Wilson lying in state. Above it was the headline: Editor Wilson Back Home—To Stay.

Hank Klibanoff is Sunday editor of the Philadelphia Inquirer. *He is working on a book with Gene Roberts about the news coverage of the civil rights movement in the South.*

Part 2

TODAY

9

Letizia Battaglia

*Her Photographs Awakened Awareness
of the Sicilian Mafia.*

Alexander Stille

LETIZIA BATTAGLIA BEGAN to photograph the Sicilian Mafia in 1974, long before it was popular, chic, convenient or particularly safe to do so. As the photography director of *L'Ora*, Palermo's left-wing daily newspaper, she or one of her assistants was present at the scene of every major crime in Palermo until shortly before the paper folded in 1990. During that period, a new, bloody ruling group within Cosa Nostra, the Mafia of the town of Corleone, wiped out the traditional bosses of Palermo and those most closely connected to them, conducting a war of extermination that cost the lives of about 1,000 people.

On call from morning until late at night, Battaglia sometimes found herself at the scene of four or five different murders in a single day. In the course of this difficult, grisly, often profoundly unpleasant routine, Battaglia and her long-time partner Franco Zecchin produced many of the iconic images that have come to represent Sicily and the Mafia throughout the world: a corpse lying face down in an alleyway; a boy with his face hidden in a nylon stocking brandishing a weapon—the gun is a toy, but the look on the child's face is that of a hardened killer; a group of black-shawled women sitting impassively on chairs in the presence of a corpse bleeding onto the sidewalk.

"For years, I photographed dead bodies," Battaglia said. "We felt humiliated, a people crushed and humiliated by this tragedy of Mafia," she said.

Battaglia lives in the old historic district of Palermo—a desperately poor and largely abandoned section that encapsulates the best and worst of one of the most fascinating and beautiful cities in Europe. It was once the center of the Palermo aristocracy, and its grand 17th- and 18th-century churches and palaces—filled with elaborate gilded stucco work and frescoed ceilings—are among the great expressions of baroque architecture in the world.

Battaglia is a short, rather petite woman, with shoulder-length blond hair and a pretty, delicately featured face. She wears informal, loose-fitting clothes and sandals and uses no make-up. Her hair is generally a little disheveled, held in place by her glasses, as if she was too busy to be bothered with her appearance. Although she is now 64 and her figure has filled out with age, she seems much younger: her highly animated face and bright, lively eyes give her an almost girlish quality, the air of a restless person in constant motion, constantly open to new experience. She looks like, and is, a creature of the 1960s, which, in Italy, came late but then lasted throughout the 1970s and formed her personal and political makeup. Battaglia, meaning "battle," is a name of Dickensian appropriateness in her case: she has fought innumerable political battles in Palermo, demonstrating against the Mafia, against American cruise missiles on Sicilian soil, against countless ugly development projects; in favor of the environment, feminism, the mentally ill, the gypsies and the latest wave of North African immigrants landing in Palermo.

Her decision to live in the old center of Palermo is, like most things in Battaglia's life, a political decision. The abandonment of historic Palermo is an important part of what has been called "The Sack of Palermo." In the 1950s and '60s, Mafia-controlled real estate developers put up innumerable high-rise apartment houses in the newer part of the city leading toward the airport, while the old center was allowed literally to crumble about the ears of its citizens. The policy of willful neglect had the effect of depopulating the city center and forcing all but the very poorest people to leave the old downtown for the new high rises. By moving downtown, Battaglia has gambled her money and her life on the revival of Palermo.

WHEN BATTAGLIA STARTED her photographic work, people regarded the

Mafia as a purely criminal and local problem. Some even romanti-cized it. Anti-Mafia demonstrations in the 1970s were sparsely at-tended with most citizens closing their shutters in fear. But attitudes changed in the course of Battaglia's career, in part because of deadly changes within the Mafia itself. In 1974, (the year Battaglia became photo director of *L'Ora*) there were only eight deaths by heroin over-dose in all of Italy, but by the early 1990s there were more than 1,000 a year. The Sicilian Mafia, along with becoming the chief conduit of heroin between Asia and the United States, had decided to develop its own domestic market as well, creating an epidemic with a hard-core addict population of more than 200,000 in less than a decade. The drug trade attracted a public outcry, but as police and prosecutors tried to crack down on it they began to be killed with astonishing regularity. Between 1978 and 1992, the Sicilian Mafia murdered virtually every public official who interfered with its business—police officers, judges, prosecutors, mayors, members of parliament, the head of the chief governing party, the head of the chief opposition party, the general in charge of the military police and even the governor of Sicily.

Battaglia documented virtually all of these dismal events. The pow-erful images she created gave faces and corporeal reality to and helped awaken public awareness of a phenomenon that was tragically ignored for decades to the detriment of Sicily and Italy as a whole. The stories that accompanied those pictures have yellowed and faded, but her photographs have remained remarkably fresh and powerful.

As the political assassinations multiplied, people began to under-stand the importance of politics to Mafia business and the crucial role of political protection in enabling the Mafia's ability to kill with impu-nity. As the political dimension of the Mafia began to become more and more evident, the crowds at anti-Mafia demonstrations got larger and louder. By the 1990s, the citizens of Palermo pelted their leaders with coins and demanded justice. Battaglia's photographs and her own entrance in politics played a role in the transformation of public con-sciousness.

One morning in 1993, Italian police turned up at Battaglia's front door with a warrant to examine her archives, asking to look through her files of the Christian Democratic Party—the party that ruled Sicily and Italy for virtually the entire post World War II period. Prosecutors were beginning to investigate the political ties of the Sicilian Mafia, and Battaglia's photographs would prove invaluable in reconstructing who was sitting next to whom at certain key moments and events. Along with shooting crime scenes, Battaglia had photographed virtually everything of possible interest to the newspaper—fashion shows, religious processions, street scenes, striptease shows, wedding banquets and political rallies. Taking hundreds of shots a day for nearly 20 years, Battaglia had accumulated some 600,000 images—most of which remain in negatives and contact sheets—creating an extraordinary visual chronicle of Sicily over the years.

Sicily was a political stronghold for the Christian Democrats. During the Cold War, when the Christian Democrats and their allies played a major role in blocking the Italian Communist Party's rise to power, organized crime played a significant role in intimidating radical forces on the island. Between 1945 and 1955, 43 Socialists or Communists were murdered in Sicily, generally around election time. Unfortunately, the dependence of the governing parties grew even as the tensions of the Cold War began to lessen. By the 1970s, the Christian Democrats' support had dropped below 30 percent in most of northern Italy, while they routinely collected more than 45 percent in southern places such as Palermo.

Under those conditions, it became difficult to get rid of local political bosses who were rumored to have organized crime connections but could deliver the vote. Battaglia shot a series of photographs of Vito Ciancimino, the former Christian Democratic mayor and former barber of Corleone—rumored for many years to be "in the pocket" of Salvatore "Totò" Riina, the boss of bosses of the Sicilian Mafia. Battaglia took a series of rather chilling photographs of Ciancimino laughing jovially as an honored guest at various Christian Democratic Party gatherings, at a time when his Mafia connections were supposed to have made him persona non grata in government circles. Among them are photographs of Ciancimino with Salvatore Lima, another former mayor of Palermo and Prime Minister Giulio Andreotti's chief political supporter in Sicily.

Investigators also found a photograph from the late 1970s of Andreotti himself with a Sicilian businessman named Nino Salvo, who was later found to have been one of the linchpins of the Mafia system in Sicily. Salvo had been one of the biggest financial supporters of the Christian Democratic Party in Sicily as well, apparently, a "made" Mafia member who acted as the principal go-between for Cosa Nostra's dealings with its friends in government. Andreotti had always strenuously denied ever having met Salvo. But two photographs in Battaglia's archive showed them together on the occasion of a Christian Democratic rally in Sicily. Salvo, in fact, hosted a big reception after the rally at his luxurious Hotel Zagarella outside Palermo. In a photograph of the event from Battaglia's archive, Salvo is seen greeting Andreotti. (Andreotti insists that even if he met Salvo, he does not recall it.)

Battaglia herself had forgotten having taken the photograph. Its potential significance was apparent only 15 years after it was taken. Andreotti was eventually acquitted of collusion with the Mafia because, other than the testimony of Mafia turn-coats, the photograph is the only piece of hard, physical evidence directly linking Andreotti to a known Mafia member. Yet the Andreotti photograph illustrates dramatically the historic value of Battaglia's work, which visually documents a time and place of critical importance in contemporary Italian history.

WHEN BATTAGLIA STARTED her work, a woman photographer was not especially welcome, particularly at the scene of a crime. "I always had problems with the police, with the family of the victims," she said. At a certain point, she began receiving anonymous letters with death threats. She took them to Giovanni Falcone, the top Mafia prosecutor in Palermo during the 1980s, who advised her to stop working for a few months. She decided to continue and, fortunately, nothing happened.

It was not always easy to tell what sort of photograph might touch a delicate nerve. One day, Battaglia was photographing a striptease show when the proprietors became extremely angry and threatening. When she refused to give them the roll of film she had shot, arguing that it contained frames from a previous shoot, they put her in a car and drove her back to her studio. "They took me into the darkroom and forced me to develop the film and cut out the few miserable shots that I had taken," she said. "I called the police, but they decided to do nothing." To this day, Battaglia does not know what she saw that day that she shouldn't have. "For years every morning when I stepped outside, I was afraid," she said.

At one point, she incurred the wrath of one of the most dangerous Mafiosi in Sicily, Leoluca Bagarella—brother-in-law of Totò Riina himself and considered one of the bloodiest killers in all of Cosa

Nostra. When Battaglia began to photograph him after his arrest in the early 1980s, Bagarella tried to break free and attack her. Battaglia held her ground and produced a famous photograph of Bagarella that captured all his rage and ferocity.

"It took a number of years before I was seen in a positive light, that I was not just some kind of cop with a camera," she said. "They saw that I didn't just take pictures of the dead, that I returned to take pictures of the poverty and the conditions of life in Palermo. People would call out to me: 'Come, my roof needs fixing.'"

Battaglia's pictures of ordinary Palermo life are an important complement to her Mafia reportage. Her many photographs of religious processions—one of a woman crawling up the stairs of the church on her knees is a memorable example—render something of the tragic sense of life in Sicily. The Sicilians have lived under the yoke of oppressive rulers from the Greeks, Romans, Arabs, Normans and Spanish to the Mafia. The fervent hopes in the hereafter and the intensity of religious passion seem to represent a redemption from a world of almost uninterrupted hardship and suffering. Death has always loomed large in Sicilian culture and il giorno dei morti (Day of the Dead) is as important in Sicily as Christmas is in other parts of Europe.

And these worlds come together with startling power in the images that define Battaglia's Sicily. Perhaps the most striking example of this is Battaglia's extraordinary image of a murder victim with an image of Christ wearing a crown of thorns tattooed upon his back. Similarly, in a picture of a funeral after a Mafia killing, the image of a dark-faced widow is reflected in the back window of a hearse.

Another exceptional Battaglia photograph that illuminates the dark side of Sicilian life is the photograph of the dying horse. The scene is from an illegal horse race, one of many such races in which the horses are frequently crippled or injured because there is no supervision or regulation. What is remarkable in the image is the total indifference of the crowd to the presence of this mortally wounded animal, who, having broken its leg, will soon have to be shot. The picture shows the corrosive effect of the small and large illegalities that pervade Sicilian life. The fact that so many live outside of the normal parameters of the law—selling contraband cigarettes, counterfeit tapes or watches, operating stores or stalls without a license, living in houses that were built against the zoning laws or simply underreporting their income and evading taxes—places millions of Sicilians outside the law, making them afraid of the legal authorities and natural accomplices to the Mafia.

Equally important and interesting are Battaglia's photographs of the Palermo aristocracy. Of special note is the photograph of Palazzo Ganci, home of the princes of San Vincenzo, used in the making of Luchino Visconti's famous film "The Leopard." The glitter of the palace assumes a sinister air of decay when one considers that the young prince himself was arrested in a Mafia roundup. On the day he was arrested, there was a big reception at which much of Palermo high society would be in attendance. Despite the arrest, the prince's mother insisted on going, Battaglia recalls: "'Nothing's happened,' the mother said. 'Nothing's happened.' We had an aristocracy and a bourgeoisie that was often the accomplice of the Mafia."

GRADUALLY THE KILLINGS of the 1980s—and the courageous response of a new generation of Palermo magistrates—began to erode the attitudes of indifference, collusion and omertà (code of silence). And a new generation of anti-Mafia politicians emerged. Battaglia joined the small environmental Green Party and became a member of the Palermo City Council in 1985. She spent years fighting a massive development project that would have resulted in the paving over of large parts of the coastline near Palermo. It turned out that the lead developer, who was later arrested, confessed to having relations with the Mafia as well as distributing bribes to politicians to win approval for the project. In the years of trying to defeat the project, Battaglia watched (and photographed) as the developer, Benedetto D'Agostino, was courted and befriended by the most powerful politicians of the city, riding around in fleets of yachts equipped with bathroom faucets made of gold. She even photographed his wedding, where the best man was none other than Salvatore Lima, the former mayor of Palermo, whose status as Andreotti's chief political supporter in Sicily suggested a range of political and criminal connections.

In 1992, Lima was himself killed in a Mafia hit in Palermo—a sign of a breakdown in the traditional alliances that had supported Mafia power in Sicily. With increased public pressure to crack down on crime, it became impossible for the Mafia's friends in power to continue protecting it. The Mafia lashed out at the prosecutors who were most effective in combating Cosa Nostra, Giovanni Falcone and Paolo Borsellino, both of whom were blown up by car bombs during the

summer of 1992. The public outrage that followed helped bring about
a general housecleaning in Italian life and prompted the first serious
investigations into the relations between Mafia and politics. It also
brought a return to power in Palermo of Battaglia's good friend and
political ally Leoluca Orlando, a maverick Christian Democrat and
opponent of the Mafia who had been mayor of Palermo for a brief
time in the late 1980s.

IN HER POLITICAL CAREER, Battaglia has worked for simple, practical
things, like cleaning the city, trying to reverse decades of neglect, in
which the garbage collection system, like so much else in the city, was
a means of distributing patronage no-show jobs and siphoning money
to Mafia-controlled subcontractors. "They didn't clean the city, and
the Palermitans, seeing that the garbage wasn't collected, in a spirit of
perversity, made it even dirtier. They have never loved government
and never believed in the people governing them. They would keep
their houses spotless but dump garbage just outside the door. I made
some incredible scenes in this city," Battaglia said.

One episode that Battaglia recalls with particular fondness occurred
when she set about trying to clean a small park in one of the poorest,
most Mafia-infested neighborhoods in the city. "The park is near a
very old and beautiful bridge, but all these trucks were parked all
around so that you could not see either the park or the bridge. I went
to the shopkeepers who owned the trucks and asked them if they could
park somewhere else. 'Signora, you want to ruin us,' they said. 'I'm
just trying to make the neighborhood more attractive.'" Battaglia announced that she was going to sit there until the trucks moved. "I sat
on the sidewalk all day. My workers tried to get me to leave. Then at a
certain point, one of the owners said: 'Signora, you are going to ruin
us, but we will move the trucks.' They understood that I was there for
them, that I was not there to get money or votes. They decided to give
up a personal advantage for a collective good. It was a sublime moment."

It would be a gross exaggeration to say that Palermo has rid itself of
either the Mafia or its centuries-old problems. Unemployment in the
city, as in much of southern Italy, is still over 20 percent. The Mafia,
although under great pressure from countless arrests and trials, is still
very much alive. While heroin trafficking has been seriously disrupted,
the Mafia has reacted, according to numerous recent investigations, by

tightening its grip on storekeepers paying protection. But Palermo is unquestionably a cleaner and safer and better-run city than it was 10 or 20 years ago. With Mafia killings no longer front-page news, Battaglia is now looking for other subjects for her work. She feels that a certain cycle of Palermo life has ended—perhaps for the better. "Maybe the Mafia is no longer photographable," she said. "Things have changed."

Alexander Stille is author of Excellent Cadavers: The Mafia and the Death of the First Italian Republic.

10

Picturing Breast Cancer

Matuschka and Ned Asta

Interviewed by Betty Rollin

While the courage of journalists is honored with prizes and awards, the courage of sources is less widely recognized. The gap is particularly noticeable in photography, where pictures of people in the most dire of circumstances can appear with little appreciation for what placed them in front of a camera and how the experience shaped their lives.

In this interview, Betty Rollin—a journalist, author and breast cancer survivor—talks with two women who revealed their own scars from cancer treatment. Matuschka's picture appeared on the cover of The New York Times Magazine *on August 15, 1993. The picture of Ned Asta appeared in* The Ithaca (N.Y.) Journal *on October 18, 1997.*

Matuschka

MSJ: How did it happen? How did the picture come to be?

Matuschka: First I gathered all the pictures on the market of women who had breast cancer and how they dealt with it. And I didn't like the way they dealt with it because they had their hands over their face or their heads had been cut off or there was [turning] this.

MSJ: These were pictures of women who were naked, but they were kind of hiding themselves.

Matuschka: Right. Well, first I hid too. I was in the dressing room of a clothing store after my mastectomy, and I was cowering in the corner. But then I thought, "Am I going to have to hide like this for the rest of my life?" I thought, "No, let's try to show what a mastectomy looks like to the rest of the world."

MSJ: Was this partly for your own head or were you in a do-good mode or both?

Matuschka: Well, it was both. I did my own photographs of myself and put slogans on the photographs—although *The New York Times* picture didn't put slogans. My slogans said "Time for Prevention" or "Medicine Without Logic." You know, they used to say it is nothing to worry about if you came in with a tumor. So I had a picture of me bald with no breasts and with a sign, "Nothing to Worry About."

MSJ: I understand you are an artist—you do that—but, still, did you have any fear of exposing yourself in this way?

Matuschka: Well, I had a fear that I would go unrecognized, and all this work would be for naught.

MSJ: What were you trying to say with your pictures and with the one that wound up in the Times?

Matuschka: That if a woman does have breast cancer, does have her breast removed, she is capable of sensuality, pride, dignity, and she is no less of a woman because her breast was removed.

MSJ: Matuschka, when you look at photographs of yourself, do you see them as beautiful even with the breast removed, or do you see them as just "this is how it is?"

Matuschka: Well, I see it, "this is how it is." But my pictures are very orchestrated towards a beauty result. These pictures are posed, lit—they are not documentary images. Like the reason the cover on The New York Times was so beautiful was that a tremendous amount of consideration went into that picture. A dress was designed specifically to be cut away. I had light coming in from the fire escape, beaming in. I really was revealing myself as a metaphor for other women, as an advertisement for breast cancer. To make the ad acceptable in this country it had to be beautiful.

MSJ: And in your mind, what kind of an advertisement was it?

Matuschka: That breast cancer was an epidemic. It was a serious issue that needed much more attention—medically, politically, socially, scientifically, financially.

MSJ: So you wanted to shock people into awareness.

Matuschka: Yeah, though I didn't think it was going to be such a shock. I was living with a mastectomy, and my mother had had a mastectomy so it wasn't shocking for me.

MSJ: How exactly did the photograph end up in *The New York Times?*

Matuschka: It was just a fluke. I was at the National Breast Cancer Coalition and they refused to let me put my pictures up on the walls. So I decided to wear them. I started walking around the convention with my pictures on, like, a sandwich board. And someone from *The New York Times* came up to me because she was covering the convention. Afterwards, the *Times* called me up and wanted to see my portfolio. This was very funny because first they said we are doing an article, but we can't show any breasts. They changed their minds.

MSJ: What was the best that came of this?

Matuschka: It gave an impetus to the breast cancer movement. It also helped women who have had mastectomies. One of the best quotes was, "Finally a cover girl that looks like me." So I think it helped people who already had breast cancer, and it helped men deal with their wives.

MSJ: Did you get the reaction you expected to get?

Matuschka: This is how naive I was: I thought no one is interested in the picture; it is August. Everyone is on vacation. People don't take things seriously in the summer. But my phone did not stop ringing for six months, and I mean not stop ringing—women who have had breast cancer, television programs, groups, wanting to use my picture, publications wanting to use my picture.

What it did do that I don't like is that oftentimes doctors would show this picture to women promoting mastectomy, and I don't like that. Because they are basically saying, "Hey, she did it. No big deal." Well, it is a big deal having your breast removed. Especially if you don't need your breast removed. You know, a lot of breast cancers don't need to be treated that way.

MSJ: So the down side, in a way, is that it was too successful.

Matuschka: In some ways. But it did make women go for early detection more, women who didn't want to end up looking like me, with a chest like me.

MSJ: Did you get any negative reactions?

Matuschka: Some. Letters and phone calls, like, "How dare you, you should be sued. I have been concealing my breast, my mastectomy, from my husband for 25 years, and now you go and show what a mastectomy looks like after I have been concealing it," which was precisely my point.

MSJ: I am interested in your history. How did you get to be the bold person who did what you did?

Matuschka: Any kind of heroism that I wanted to copy came from my father. My father was a police officer on the George Washington Bridge, and I remember there was a rash in the '60s of people jumping off the bridge. And my father saved a bunch of people from jumping off the bridge and he was considered a hero. I was very impressed with his heroism.

Also, I always wanted to help others because I had so much help when I was a teen-ager. My mother died of breast cancer when I was 13, and I left home soon after. I moved to New York. And basically I had this pioneering spirit. I was rehabilitated by the state of New Jersey, and I was adopted by this foster family. If it wasn't for these people, I would have perished in the drug scene.

MSJ: And how do you feel today about yourself and what you have done? .

Matuschka: Good. But even with all the activism, all the stuff that I have done, the hardest time I have, believe it or not, is in the gym. In the women's locker room. That is when I am the most alienated. That is when I get these looks that I can't stand. That is when people do not embrace me.

I have fewer problems with men, which is really ironic. You would think it would be the opposite.

MSJ: Interesting. Does it concern you that some women might see you and shudder and then not get their mammogram and not go for the surgery?

Matuschka: I think there will be some women that this will basically help. But you can't help everybody, and I think it is better to expose the truth than conceal it.

MSJ: But I am wondering, does it bother you in the locker room when you have a sense that you are upsetting people?

Matuschka: I think they are upsetting me. I actually had a bad dream about it. I dreamt that I locked everybody out of the locker room.

MSJ: I think I can interpret that dream!

Matuschka: I look at it like, "Why should I have to hide for the rest of my life?"

MSJ: Do you think that part of what may offend people is something new and strange, and if more people did what you did then it wouldn't be that strange?

Matuschka: Right. On the other hand, it was very interesting: a bunch of older women wrote that after they saw me do this, they went on the beach one-breasted, and these are older women. They took photographs and sent them to me saying, "I would have never been able to do this prior to you coming out and doing it." And they walk around proud now and they feel, "Why should I conceal myself?"

MSJ: That must make you feel good.

Matuschka: The whole thing changed my life in so many different ways. It gave me focus. I got to see how art and activism and politics can actually effect change. The fact that I was able to help other women either save their breasts or have early detection or look at alternatives or whatever makes me feel really good. And to be an artist and have actually been recognized in my lifetime is an amazing feat. I am not talking about being a major artist who makes a lot of money, I am talking about being the grass-roots artist that I was.

MSJ: So you must feel proud of yourself.

Matuschka: I definitely feel proud that I did it and definitely grateful I had the opportunity and I came on the scene at the right time. Looking back at it, I am really glad I chose the moment.

Ned Asta

MSJ: What made you pose for this photograph?

Ned Asta: I was devastated when the breast was removed, and ashamed, and to tell you the truth when I saw Matuschka, I thought, "That is amazing," and she gave me courage. But I just think exposing it is the way I wanted to go.

I was angry also. I was, like, "Look, this happened to me. Do you want to see it?" That might not be a good attitude but . . .

MSJ: No, I think anger plays a role with all of us. You are not alone there. What was your situation when cancer hit you?

Asta: It was 1993. After they had biopsied it, I went to the surgeon's office. He was very nice but it was, "I hate to tell you this, Ned, but you have cancer." And I just was dumbfounded. And being that I am into my own body—I have always loved my body—I was devastated.

I said, "Do you mind if I go to other doctors?" I went all over New York state, and they all said the same thing: "Infiltrating carcinoma. And we've got to take your whole breast off."

MSJ: And what was the space between the surgery and the time that you decided to do this photo.

Asta: Let me see, my kid was 6—at least three to four years later.

MSJ: And how did it come about?

Asta: I helped start Ithaca Breast Cancer Alliance. It was a grass-roots thing. Someone on *The Ithaca Journal* said, "We are doing a whole pull-out section. Is there anyone willing to show us a mastectomy?" Right away I got the phone calls. They knew I would do that, because of my personality and also being in ACT UP and having a lot of friends die of AIDS—that helped me.

MSJ: I see. You warmed to that idea right away?

Asta: Right away—they knew what I would say, and no one else wanted to do it. Even the young ones didn't want to do it.

MSJ: You didn't have any hesitation?

Asta: Okay, the hesitation I had, I must tell you, is my son. My son is in the community and was going to the local elementary school, and he was the only one that I was concerned about—no one else. I just thought, "Would he be harassed?" It was in the local paper and would the parents say, "Oh, my God, that's Ned's son"? So I had to clear it with him.

MSJ: What did your son say?

Asta: First he said, "I don't know, Mommy," and we talked about it slowly. I said, "If my picture is in the local paper naked, I want to show people what happens when you have breast cancer and how we could prevent it." I told him about early detection. I actually explained it to him. And he said he loved me and that he would be proud of me.

MSJ: And how old was he at the time?

Asta: He was 9.

MSJ: He was 9 at the time. So he showed some courage too.

Asta: He totally did. Yes, he did.

MSJ: So once your son said do it, then you were absolutely sure you wanted to go ahead.

Asta: Yeah, it was no problem to me.

MSJ: Really? That surprises me, I suppose, because of my own memories about what it was like to lose a breast. What happened to your vanity?

Asta: After I first had my mastectomy, I didn't want anyone to see me naked. So for the first time I started wearing my bathing suit where I swim. The worst thing was when I would go for a sauna at the gym. I would put a towel over my scar. Over my missing breast. I was embarrassed. That was in the beginning.

But when the photographer from *The Ithaca Journal* asked me to do this, I just thought to jump over this feeling of being embarrassed, to jump over this feeling of pain. I just felt, "I am going to show everybody. If it scares people, I am sorry."

MSJ: Was it a little bit—correct me if I am wrong—sort of thumbing your nose at what had happened to you?

Asta: Yes, . . . yes. A little bit: "I am sorry that this happened to me, this is horrible but I want to help you. I don't want it to scare you that much but I want to show you."

MSJ: I want to show you so that you will what?

Asta: You will do a self-exam. You will not wait for that mammogram.

MSJ: So you wanted in a sense to say, "Look at this awful thing, and be sure it doesn't happen to you." Is that the message?

Asta: Yes.

MSJ: Were you also saying it is not so bad? Was it a mix?

Asta: It was definitely a mix. The scar is very neat. It is a good job [laughs]. So I was, "I have a breast on my left side and one is missing on my right side, and I am going ahead." In a way, I was trying to make a quick friendship with the whole world here in Ithaca in saying, "I am going on, and you can go on."

And not only that but, "We will fight, and we have this organization and we will raise money for research."

MSJ: And what effect did it have? What happened when the picture was published?

Asta: Well, I work in a restaurant. I am a host and I am a cashier and I own it with 19 other people. And it was constant—people were just coming through the door and shaking my hand, and, "My God, you are brave." And also I wear tight blouses where my left breast shows and my right one doesn't, and one woman came up to me and says, "My husband and I are sitting here and we realize that you are Ned, and we just want to thank you. And I have had a mastectomy too and I haven't been rebuilt either."

MSJ: And why have you not done reconstruction?

Asta: Because I am scared. I think I am a little behind the times with that because they must have great implants by now, and I am just really scared of surgery. That is a part of me that is immature.

MSJ: Did you have any negative response when the photograph was published?

Asta: This is really amazing: nobody gave me a negative response.

MSJ: Did you worry that some women might look at this picture and be horrified and . . .

Asta: Yes.

MSJ: . . . and rather than help them, they might say, "I am not getting my mammogram; I am not getting a checkup; I'm just going to run and hide because I don't want this to happen to me"?

Asta: I don't think I concentrated on that but I must say in the paper they cautioned readers: "When you come to Section Two, you might not want your children to see this." I didn't think that it would scare people until the editor said, "If you don't want your children to see this. . . . "

MSJ: Let me ask you a hard question, Ned.

Asta: Sure.

MSJ: Would you say you did this primarily for yourself or primarily for others?

Asta: Oh, my God, that is such a good question. I know that my ego was involved, and I didn't think about it much, I took action. I do that a lot. So I think maybe I am going to have to say, I did it for myself first and then people second.

MSJ: I think that is an honest answer, and I think that would be the case for many people, whether they admit it or not. With First, You Cry, I have been given a lot of points for it over the years, but I know I was doing it for myself. At first it didn't occur to me that it might help anybody else.

Asta: And, of course, it did.

MSJ: Yes, but for me that was just a great and a surprising bonus! But you were thinking of others, even at the start. So do you feel that you were courageous?

Asta: I don't know. I have always been political since the '60s. You know, it was anti-war, it was abortions, it was AIDS and then all of a sudden I said, "Here comes breast cancer." I felt like in a way it is my duty.

MSJ: Still, it couldn't have been easy to do. Was it?

Asta: To tell you the truth, I was sweating and I was nervous before [the photographer] walked in the door. But going back to Matuschka, I thought, "If she can do it, why can't I? Why can't I do this for New York upstate?"

MSJ: Was there a pleasure simply in the truth telling about it? Did it make you feel good to just . . .

Asta: Yes, yes, the word that you said, "truth telling." It was like, "Here it is, this is the truth. I have gone through this and it is the truth."

MSJ: Time played a role here; it sounds like you might not have wanted to do this photograph in the first year.

Asta: Not at all. You are totally right. That is when I was crying and hiding in the showers. I was mortified at the beginning.

MSJ: So the courage to do this came after your own adjustment to this new body.

Asta: Yes, totally—and let me tell you it also came from seeing other women that have one breast or no breast. I went to two huge breast cancer retreats, and that just changed my life. Period. Seeing other women sit in the sauna with one breast made me think, "Okay, we can do this. We can do this."

MSJ: And you did.

Asta: Yes!

Betty Rollin is a contributing correspondent for NBC News and PBS's "Religion and Ethics Newsweekly." She is author of First, You Cry *and* Last Wish.

11

Great Courage, Small Places

When People Believe their Work Matters

Eric Newton and Mary Ann Hogan

WHITESBURG, KENTUCKY, 1974—They have to get the paper out this week, have to. Publishers Tom and Pat Gish see it as taking care of business. The office of their scrappy mining-town weekly, *The Mountain Eagle*, has just been drenched with kerosene and set on fire, punishment a local cop meted out for the sin of writing about police harassment. But that isn't going to stop them from getting the paper out.

The *Eagle*'s motto—"It Screams!"—is a fitting battle cry for the tiny family-owned enterprise. Since the 1960s, The *Eagle* has stood up to corruption, bad cops and politicians and, most notably, strip miners whose bulldozers, in their search for coal, have plowed up family cemetery plots and sent caskets along with boulders and trees down hillsides into rivers and people's homes.

The ruined *Eagle* office is just another obstacle. The Gishes are used to obstacles. That's the nature of small-town news, Tom Gish says again and again. "It is hard to be loved and to advocate change in the community at the same time," he tells a press association gathering many years later. "We all like to think our readers like for us to keep them informed, but often the response is more like, 'Kill the messenger.'"

In the week in question in 1974, with the help of family and friends,

99

Tom and Pat Gish publish the next edition from their living room. That week, the *Eagle*'s motto reads, "It Still Screams!"

Here in the home of the brave, storytellers tend to go so soppy over dramatic acts of fearlessness. Journalists venerate the heroes of their profession, their feats and sacrifices—Tom Paine doing jail time for unleashing revolutionary ideas, Elijah Lovejoy dying in the fight against slavery, William Allen White enduring endless ridicule for championing free expression.

Journalism enshrines their efforts with awards bearing their names. We cheer their moral strength from the sidelines, secretly praying for one sliver of their mettle, just a spark of the spirit that bore them into the pantheon.

In a strange way, this lets us off the hook, the notion that courage is a thing for kings, martyrs and news Olympians.

It gives us a great excuse for not trying—*How could we possibly measure up?* In truth, however, many of the greatest acts of journalistic courage come from the smallest places. A mining town. An Indian reservation. An urban neighborhood. More often than not, they are mounted by everyday folk, rooted in everyday events. Meeting a deadline. Asking a question. Taking care of business.

Call them simple everyday acts of conscience—but ones that, in retrospect, grow into greatness. They help us remember that courageous acts don't require earthquakes, civil wars or killing fields. They show us that journalistic courage can surface anywhere people believe their work really matters.

IN THE EARLY 1990s, work really matters—it means survival—for Bob and Nancy Maynard, owner-publishers of *The Oakland Tribune*. They are embarked on one of the ultimate newspaper fixer-upper jobs, rebuilding their daily into an instrument for community good. The challenge, one among dozens, comes in the form of an ad for handguns. It's 1992. The murder rate in Oakland is rising. A local gun dealer advertises sports weapons in a number of the region's papers but saves his handgun and assault-weapon ads for the Trib. Revenue from the gun ads means $100,000 a year, a small gold mine for the limping but plucky newspaper.

The Maynards ask the dealer to keep the sports weapons but drop the street weapons. The dealer cancels his ads altogether, just as the publishers feared he would. But "it was an integrity issue," Nancy Maynard says eight years later. "We couldn't advertise handguns and assault weapons and at the same time editorialize against them."

For some, journalistic courage may mean putting truth ahead of comfort or even safety. For publishers, it usually means putting truth ahead of money—in this case, six months' worth of ad money, which is what the Trib loses before the gun dealer agrees to resume advertising with the paper with just the sports guns.

"This was not a frivolous decision," Maynard says. "During that time, when Tuesday at 3 a.m. of payroll week rolled around, you lay there and wondered how much cash was available. That was the level of intensity. We really needed every dollar we could get.

"It's just that some dollars are too expensive."

Sam Lacy, sports editor of the *Baltimore Afro-American*, finds the challenge in the form of an obvious—but in the 1930s, undebated—question: if ball players in the baseball Negro Leagues are as agile and strong and home-run hitting as the white players in the major leagues, why no black players in the majors?

A one-time Negro League pitcher himself, Lacy seeks answers as he sets out to "break down the barriers that stand between the dark-skinned diamonder of merit and a place on the payroll" of major league clubs. And in 1948, the man who has been covering the integration of baseball for a decade draws the assignment of a lifetime: to follow Jackie Robinson's first year with the Brooklyn Dodgers.

The sports editor rooms with the famous Dodger rookie in "colored" hotels. Throughout the south, Lacy faces his own set of obstacles. He is not allowed in stadium press boxes. In Florida, one ballpark won't let him in at all. (Robinson sneaks him in through a loose floorboard.) Even so, the *Afro* tells the best story—the whole story—of Robinson's barrier-breaking year.

Half a century later, at age 94, as he is being inducted into the sportswriting wing of the Baseball Hall of Fame at Cooperstown, New York, for his role in integrating baseball, Sam Lacy says this about the honor, about his life: "I've always felt that there was nothing special about me, that I was not the only person who could have done what I did. Any person with a little vision, a little curiosity, a little nerve could have done what I did."

HOLLYWOOD LOVES WARTIME courage, the drama of, say, a *New York Times* reporter searching Cambodia for his lost colleague. And there's grit and grist of legend, no doubt, in Morley Safer's bringing us television of U.S. Marines torching the Vietnamese village of Cam Ne. Or in Fred Friendly's quitting as CBS News chief because the network won't air the congressional hearings on Vietnam. Or even in Walter Cronkite's famous announcement that we were "mired" in the war, and "the only rational way out will be to negotiate."

But what about all the others who stand up to the things that stand in their way? What about Ike Pappas? It's 1963, and Pappas is standing right there, in fact—in the basement of a Dallas police station—when Jack Ruby shoots Lee Harvey Oswald. Pappas has just stuck his microphone into Oswald's face, asking, "Do you have anything to say in your defense?" A second later, chaos. Ike's act of courage? "To start talking, to report it."

And what of Bill King? It's 1989 and he's a play-by-play man covering World Series game three, Oakland A's and San Francisco Giants at Candlestick Park. Then the Loma Prieta earthquake hits. The emergency broadcast system fails. Northern California is in a panic. But King is still on the air. His act of grace under pressure? He calmly reads the pages that are in all California phone books, the ones that tell exactly what everyone must do in case of a major earthquake.

Whatever the ingredient—instinct, integrity or "a little nerve"—Charlayne Hunter-Gault has it. One of two African-American journalism students entering the University of Georgia in 1961, she's greeted by racists condemning her, vowing she will never graduate. She shows up, books in hand, week after week. Her 1963 graduation inspires others black students to follow her to journalism school. Hunter-Gault's explanation: "With a passion bordering on obsession, I wanted to be a journalist."

To make a difference. Added to everything else, it becomes more than enough. Enough to drive New York *World* columnist Heywood Broun from his comfortable perch to start the Newspaper Guild. Or to push Carl T. Rowan from the *Minneapolis Tribune* to travel south to expose Jim Crow laws. Or to make Ruben Salazar abandon the safety of the *Los Angeles Times* and head back to the streets with Latino community station KMEX-TV and, ultimately, to the anti-war demonstration where he is killed by police.

MORE OFTEN THAN NOT, great courage in small places means digging into the messy landscape of one's own backyard—even if it means ending up without a home, or ending up at home in the company of enemies. *Eagle* publisher Tom Gish describes the challenge of the would-be courageous in the out-of-the-way place: "Small towns across America are dying. . . . Should the editor keep his mouth shut and his typewriter quiet? Or should he seek solutions, and through news stories, features and editorials try to awaken the town and get some movement under way?"

His words capture the lot of a handful of determined newspaper editors in the south—Hodding Carter Jr. in Greenville, Mississippi; Harry Ashmore in Little Rock, Arkansas; John Seigenthaler in Nashville, Tennessee; Ralph McGill in Atlanta—who in the 1950s and 1960s risk economic health and physical safety by talking about the need for civil rights on their own weevil-infested acreage. Or even of *Afro* sports editor Lacy, whose campaign to integrate baseball leads him to ask hard questions about the practices in his own home turf, Negro League baseball itself: bad management, teams in bed with racketeers, players jumping contracts. Was there, Lacy asks *Afro* readers, "something to the contention that we (black players) are keeping ourselves down?"

And certainly *San Francisco Chronicle* reporter Randy Shilts, who refuses to keep his mouth shut in the 1980s when he reveals the local prevalence of "baffling diseases hitting primarily gay men." Shilts, one of the first openly homosexual reporters on a major metropolitan daily, knows that the problem—first called "gay-related immuno-deficiency diseases," later known as AIDS—won't go away soon. He breaks with gay community loyalty by reporting how bathhouses and homosexual lifestyle choices can spread the killer disease. His reporting leads to his being ostracized from the inner ranks of San Francisco's large and powerful gay community, which brands Shilts as a traitor to his own kind. Villainized in the local gay press, Shilts continues reporting, gaining national prominence with his best-selling book on the epidemic, *And The Band Played On*. In 1994, Shilts dies of AIDS, after having kept his condition a secret for several years, explaining: "I didn't want to end up being an activist. I wanted to keep on being a reporter."

THE SOCIAL GEOMETRY here is fundamental: smaller people, by definition, face bigger obstacles. And so, in the end, a fitting epigraph to the great-courage, small-places pantheon might be: the less power you have, the more courage you need.

Ask that group of high school students in Dade County, Florida. In 1998, their school chief says administrators can review student publications before they go to press. There are but five of them, but the students organize rallies and mount a public campaign to protect the First Amendment rights of student journalists. The school board backs down. "We had come to appreciate journalism as [school] had taught it to us," says student Isabel Eisner.

Ask Tim Giago, the one-man crusade against corrupt tribal governments who try to squash his plans for an independent Native American press. In a 1993 editorial in *Indian Country Today*, he notes: "For years a scandal sheet filled with filth about me made the rounds. . . . If that is the price one must pay in order to bring freedom of the press to Indian country, then that is the price I must pay."

The less power you have, the more courage you need.

Ask publishers Dave and Cathy Mitchell, who in the 1970s buy *The Point Reyes Light*, circulation 1,700, in a bucolic oceanside town in Marin County, California. Starting out, Dave says, they are "not afraid of angering readers, only of boring them." But small-town living means knowing your neighbors' business, and the Mitchells' neighbor just up the coast is a communal 3,000-acre alternative life-style center called Synanon, where members shave their heads, swap mates, train children in "punk squad" practices.

The *Light* chronicles the west Marin community's concerns about Synanon, from zoning ordinance violations to the stockpiling of weapons. At one point, Synanon lawyers file lawsuits totaling $1.032 billion against the tiny weekly newspaper. In 1979, the *Light* wins a Pulitzer Prize for its Synanon investigation. The once-straightforward drug rehab center agrees to pay Dave and Cathy Mitchell $50,000 each as compensation for eight years of harassment through groundless lawsuits.

The Mitchells break up. Cathy goes on to teach. Dave moves to the big city on the tails of his David-and-Goliath triumph. At the *San Francisco Examiner*, he gets the chance of a reporting lifetime: covering the bloody events of the civil war in Guatemala. "But it went without a ripple," Mitchell tells *Editor & Publisher* years later. "Nothing changed in Guatemala. My story did not affect anything. My God, in Point Reyes Station, if the postmaster is on the carpet for poor mail service, it's a big story and something is done about it."

Mitchell leaves the *Examiner*, returning to bucolic Point Reyes and his old newspaper.

"I have the enormous feeling," he says, "that what I do on the *Light* matters."

Eric Newton, news historian of The Freedom Forum's Newseum, is editor of Crusaders, Scoundrels, Journalists. *Mary Ann Hogan was the primary writer for both the Newseum's news history gallery and* Crusaders, Scoundrels, Journalists.

12

Glasnost Betrayed

In Russia, Many Conform, Few Resist.

Emma Gray

ON JUNE 8, 1998, the body of a middle-aged woman was discovered in a pond on a lonely stretch of ground on the outskirts of the city of Elista, capital of the southern autonomous republic of Kalmykia in the Russian Federation. The body had a fractured skull and multiple knife wounds. The brave voice of Larisa Yudina, a prominent newspaper editor and political activist, had finally been silenced.

The night before she was murdered, Yudina had received a phone call from a man offering documents that he promised would assist her investigation of corrupt business practices by regional officials. She agreed to meet the alleged source and left her apartment in her slippers, never to be seen alive again.

Yudina had frequently been harassed and threatened for her exposés of local corruption and hard-line rule by the millionaire president of Kalmykia, Kirsan Ilyumzhinov. Her newspaper, *Sovietskaya Kalmykia Segodnya* was the only alternative news outlet in the republic, and, as well as her role as reporter and editor, Yudina was a local leader of the liberal opposition Yabloko Party.

Yudina's death sent shock waves throughout Russia and beyond. Seven years after the breakup of the Soviet Union was heralded as a great triumph of freedom over tyranny, another journalist was murdered for doing her job. Since 1990, more than 30 Russian reporters have died in the course of practicing their profession. Many have been killed in the cross fire in the conflicts that have ravaged the Soviet Union as it split into smaller states, especially in the wars over Chechen secession. Others have been the victims of contract killings by criminal gangs, vying for the spoils as Russia embarked on its tumultuous transition to a free market.

In the drama of Russia's transformation, however, journalists like Yudina have proved to be the exception rather than the rule. She was willing to make a stand, to dig deeper for the truth even when her intimidators turned to threats and then to real physical violence. Hers is a tragic story in its own right—it is also tragic because it is such a rarity.

MANY OF YUDINA'S journalistic colleagues have capitulated. They have been won over by the forces of fear, money and cynicism. The consequences of such behavior are dire for journalism itself and for the future of democracy in Russia.

Fear is natural in a country where journalists, like all citizens, cannot rely on police protection. The lack of a functioning rule of law in Russia serves to dissuade all but the most tenacious whistle-blowers and is a wholly understandable explanation for the almost complete absence of genuine investigative reporting. The Committee to Protect Journalists monitors press freedom in Russia and the statistics make chilling reading: between 1990 and 1999, 34 journalists were killed in Russia, and hundreds were attacked. Of the deaths, the majority were killed in war zones; of those journalists who died in circumstances unrelated to military conflict, most of the murders are unsolved to this day.

A second factor is the difficult financial straits in which journalists, again like most Russians, find themselves. Pay and conditions are generally poor. Pavel Gusev, chairman of the Union of Journalists of Moscow and editor in chief of the daily *Moskovsky Komsomolets*, argues, "In circumstances of economic crisis, of unemployment, when everyone wants to eat and to live, journalists find themselves in a situation where either they must 'serve,' like a dog on its hind legs begging for a piece of meat, or be without work."

The idea of serving a master is difficult to square with the Western concept of press freedom. Whereas fear and the lure of money can and does lead many ordinary citizens to compromise, both in Russia and elsewhere, it is hoped that journalists hold themselves to a different professional standard. The idea of the media as the "Fourth Estate," acting as a watchdog of the powerful groups that seek to shape society, is firmly entrenched in countries where democracy has been in place for generations.

In Russia, that concept has been grasped by only a few. Most people—including many who work in the media—see journalism chiefly as a tool of political influence. "Very few of those who are involved in the media here are doing it as a business in the sense of pure financial gain, nor are they in the media out of a sense of civic duty," says Manana Aslamazian, general director of Internews Russia, a nonprofit organization funded by international donors that provides technical assistance to Russian broadcast media. "In our country, the main function of the media is its use as an instrument through which groups can direct their corporate policies or protect their political interests."

Journalists find themselves beholden to one or another of the political and business groups that fought over and carved up the Soviet media throughout the 1990s. There are essentially three main competing empires. They are headed by business tycoon Boris Berezovsky, who is close to the Kremlin and controls the national state television channel ORT and a number of influential newspapers; Vladimir Gusinsky, who owns NTV, the main private television station, and several publishing interests; and Yuri Luzhkov, the Moscow mayor who controls TV-Tsentr and a handful of papers.

Many Russian journalists are resigned to the task of serving one or other of the media barons who rule the airwaves and run the printing presses in Moscow and St. Petersburg. In outlying areas, local media are often answerable to the mayor or the dominant business enterprise, on whom they rely for essential services such as floor-space and computers. Some reporters serve more than one master, like Moscow-based journalist Kirill Byelyaninov, who works for both a Berezovsky newspaper and a Luzhkov television program. "This gives me a good opportunity not to waste information." he says. "I write completely different stories. I dig up dirt on both. If it's dirt on Berezovsky, I put it in the program. If it's dirt on Luzhkov, it goes in the newspaper."

POLITICIZATION OF JOURNALISM is partly a hangover from Soviet times when journalists were little more than mouthpieces for the Communist

Party. Today, reporters can choose from a vast array of outlets, but the practice of writing to promote a particular party or person has not changed. The guiding force in today's Russia tends not to be conviction or perks and privileges but money. It is widely accepted that journalists take bribes and do pieces to order (called dzhintsi after the Russian word for the once-coveted Western denim jeans). Politicians pay to be on political programs, and journalists are paid to push a particular line.

Nowhere has this been more evident than during Russia's election campaigns of the past decade. In fact, many observers point to the 1996 presidential campaign as a turning point for the press. In the early 1990s, there was an ethical quality to Russian journalism, in the tradition of the brave dissident writing that had persisted in spite of Soviet repression. Journalists like Vitaly Korotich and Artyom Borovik wrote with moral authority and were eager to instill ideals of freedom of expression in their own country.

Election campaign 1996, however, was a watershed, in which those who had been charged with the responsibility of safeguarding Russia's hard-won freedoms stumbled badly. In an open display of partisanship, much of the media promoted Boris Yeltsin. In one critical example, Igor Malashenko, then president of NTV, agreed to work simultaneously as Yeltsin's campaign manager. Malashenko argued that journalists had a duty to support the candidate who seemed most likely to protect press freedom. That sacrifice of objectivity, though understandable, is one from which Russian journalism has never truly recovered.

NTV deserves praise nonetheless for its courageous coverage of the 1994–96 Chechnya war. It won national and international acclaim for its fearless reporting from the front line and for its ability to withstand political pressure from the Kremlin. The network was threatened with the loss of its broadcasting license for transmitting dramatic pictures of the destruction of Grozny and its impact on the city's inhabitants, and for showing that the Russian forces were often made up of frightened teenage conscripts. Images such as these stimulated heated debate in the media and in society as a whole, and influenced public opinion against the war.

THE LATEST CAUCASUS campaign, however, has not inspired the same critical reporting. The second conflict was from the outset far more popular amongst the Russian people, who had been terrified by a series of apartment bombings in Moscow and elsewhere last fall, which the Kremlin blamed on Chechen separatists. The Russian government used more sophisticated propaganda techniques this time around, creating a virtual information blackout and accusing journalists who went against the official line of lacking patriotism.

NTV, in unison with almost every other media outlet, state and private, was notably muted in its criticism of the Kremlin censorship. Aslamazian of Internews Russia comments: "The current war in Chechnya and the previous one are very different from the point of view of journalists' access to information. Then, it was a question of personal courage, and having the means to pay for a vehicle or whatever. Then, you could get information from both sides. Today, the information is strictly censored, and it is clear we're being given an inaccurate picture in the media—generals in smart uniforms speak in high-flown phrases, and we don't get any information at all from the Chechen side."

One journalist who did try to get information from the Chechen side was Andrei Babitsky, a correspondent with RFE/RL's Russian Service. He ignored the Russian military's requirement for special credentials and its ban on independent travel into Chechnya without a military escort. In addition, he overcame fear of kidnappings by Chechen gangs and the nightmare of bombardment—the sound of explosions was regularly heard in his reports. Babitsky had reported independently and courageously throughout the first Chechnya war, and, unlike the majority of his colleagues, he continued the same practice during the second conflict.

Babitsky's fate became widely publicized when he vanished in Chechnya in January 2000. He was arrested and beaten by Russian forces, and released after spending more than 40 days in captivity. The reaction of Western human rights groups to his disappearance was swift and vigorous; Russian journalists, however, held back for a full month before issuing a protest. Gusev of the newspaper *Moskovsky Komsomolets* says journalists have lost their sense of solidarity: "Journalists have turned against each other, they are enemies. Everyone has a different master and these masters are fighting each other. As a result you don't have journalistic freedom, but rather individuals who are settling scores."

Another conflict that engulfs Russia is mafia wars. Investigative journalism is a dangerous occupation, whether in the arena of politics or business. The two are often intertwined, and there are copious examples of media figures who have been the victims of threats, abduction, violence and murder because they have dug too deep for someone's liking—reporters like Alexander Minkin, who works for the biweekly independent newspaper *Novaya Gazeta* and carries a gun after having been attacked twice following publication of reports that accused top-level Kremlin officials of accepting bribes. Or Alexander Khinstein of *Moskovsky Komsomolets*, who went into hiding after police, following publication of anti-corruption stories, issued him an order to accompany them to a psychiatric hospital.

MOST INVESTIGATIVE REPORTING, however, does not lead to such dire consequences. That is because there is very little that is worthy of the name: a genuine drive to get at the facts has been to a large extent replaced by slander and muckraking. Political commentator Gleb Pavlovsky says: "Investigative reporting is at a very low ebb. Plenty of compromising material is dug up, but it hasn't come about because of solid investigative reporting; it has simply been bought from the police or special services or some such organization. The press doesn't really have an investigative arm. There is compromising material, but no one investigates where it's from or whether it's true."

Such is the prevalence of compromising material that a new word has been coined, kompromat, to describe the kind of political muckraking that has become all the rage in the Russian media. Newspapers and broadcasts are full of startling revelations that usually bear little relation to reality. Riddled with inaccuracies, rarely referring to sources and often making unsubstantiated claims and accusations, the professional standard of much of the Russian media has taken a dramatic slide over the past decade.

There are significant exceptions. NTV has managed to retain a degree of critical reportage, and newspapers like Segodnya and Novaya Gazeta are bravely outspoken. Novaya Gazeta in particular continues to produce good-quality investigative reports, and the newspaper's deputy editor Sergei Sokolov is not alone in lamenting the current state of Russian journalism. "The initial euphoria of freedom which we experienced in 1991 has evaporated," he says. "Journalists feel the influence of the censor more and more. Many would like to find a niche where they could work with a measure of independence, but that, unfortunately, has proved extremely difficult. Now many have come to the conclusion that either they must stop working in their chosen profession or be much more cynical in their approach to it."

Amongst the vast profusion of media outlets in Russia today, few are dedicated to reliably informing the public and exposing wrongdoing. Part of the blame resides with the government, which has done little to create conditions in which citizens can live without fear and poverty. As regards press freedom, there has been a dramatic increase in official interference since the onset of the second Chechen war in late 1999. New laws policing the Internet and giving the authorities greater control over subsidies to thousands of newspapers across Russia also indicate a tougher Kremlin line on the media.

Part of the blame, however, falls squarely on the shoulders of the journalists themselves. Though there are individuals of great courage, many Russian journalists have sold out. If they are to stay in their profession, many see no alternative other than accepting either the role of adjunct government flack or being the mouthpiece of one of the media barons who own the airwaves. This, of course, is a great tragedy for journalists and their profession. It also bodes ill for the future of democracy in Russia.

Emma Gray is Europe program coordinator for the Committee to Protect Journalists. She is co-founder of the news agency FSN and a former producer in Moscow for Independent Television News of London and for Monitor Television.

13

Jeffrey Schmalz

Fanning a Spark of Change at **The New York Times**

Richard J. Meislin

WHEN JEFFREY SCHMALZ collapsed with a brain seizure at *The New York Times* national desk in December 1990, he was in the closet and in denial.

Like most gay people whose careers overlapped A.M. Rosenthal's tenure as the *Times'* top editor, Schmalz had hidden his sexual orientation from most of his superiors as he rose for nearly two decades through the newsroom ranks. And like a large number of gay men at that time, he had guarded himself from suspecting that he might have contracted the AIDS virus in his pursuit of an unbuttoned New York nightlife, the antithesis of his button-down, career-driven existence at the Times.

But his seizure—the result of an AIDS-related brain disease that nearly always killed its victims in months—abruptly altered that. Within weeks, all of the newsroom knew Schmalz was gay and had AIDS, and his days of hiding were over. His long-term career ambitions became irrelevant against his immediate struggle to live. And his resulting personal transformation changed Schmalz, his colleagues at the *Times* and society's view of AIDS.

Schmalz spent a year fighting his way back from the brain disease and other complications, a struggle that easily could have entitled him to live out his unknown number of remaining days at a slower pace.

115

But he needed to work; he came back to the newsroom in April 1992 and, at the suggestion of then-managing editor Joseph Lelyveld, became part of the reporting team covering the presidential campaign.

It's not clear precisely when Schmalz, who knew and loved a great story when he saw it, realized that he had to tell the one he was living. He returned to reporting in late February 1992; his first article about AIDS came in June. It recounted a session in San Francisco with Dr. Marcus Conant, and it began: "'If' is a fragile word to hang a life on, but the hundred people infected with the AIDS virus who gathered in an auditorium here on a recent night do exactly that every day: If only a cure for AIDS can be found. If only they can hold on until it is."

At that point, few beyond the *Times* knew Schmalz was writing about himself as well as others. Gradually, more of his articles dealt with issues of AIDS and the politics of gay life, showing up among more general filings from the campaign trail, and in the newsroom, the obvious questions of appropriateness and conflict of interest were quickly in play. In his memoir, Max Frankel, then the executive editor, called Schmalz "the agent of our ultimate enlightenment" in determining the balance.

"I concluded that Jeff was taking his readers deep into the world of gay politics and AIDS in forthright and revealing ways that no healthy reporter could match," Frankel wrote. "His scoops were the rarest kind, looking at the scourge from the inside out and also from the outside in."

In fact, the number of Schmalz's articles dealing with the issues of gay people and AIDS numbered only a few dozen. But his sharply drawn and humanizing portraits of the struggles and feelings of such people as the author Randy Shilts, the athlete Magic Johnson and the Republican stalwart Mary Fisher, as well as his powerful telling of the physical and emotional struggles he faced himself, resounded in the newsroom of the Times, the communities of people fighting the disease and people who might not otherwise have paid attention at all.

WHEN THE POLITICAL CAMPAIGN ended, Schmalz returned to New York and settled into a desk along a well-traveled aisle to the side of the newsroom. For many of his colleagues it was the first time they had worked side by side with—or even knew personally—someone fighting AIDS, and the scorecard of the battle was frequently evident in his personal appearance, or his presence or absence. He was an unlikely yet most obvious symbol of the changes that had come to the *Times,* and his presence and the nature of his work were ongoing encouragement for gay people in the newsroom who had only in recent years begun to relax.

Schmalz was not the first member of the *Times'* news staff to be afflicted with AIDS; that came in mid-1987, less than a year after Frankel had succeeded Rosenthal as executive editor, and only a few months after Arthur Sulzberger Jr. had become assistant publisher, bringing a more socially conscious and liberal voice to the senior executive ranks. Their compassionate treatment during the six-month illness of Robert Barrios, a promising young copy editor trainee, quietly established an encouraging precedent for those aware of it. In the years that followed, *Times* executives treated the handful of other AIDS sufferers on the news staff with discretion, concern and generous care.

Schmalz himself noted it, in a speech to gay journalists in San Francisco in June 1992. "The policy and atmosphere had begun to change under Arthur and Max long before I got sick," he said. "I was not the reason for the change; I was a beneficiary of it. It enabled me to come forward and say I was gay and had AIDS."

He credited as well the gay people who, he said, during "the scary, horrible Rosenthal years, spoke out and said they were gay at a time when people's lives at the paper were being ruined for it." They were, he said, "genuinely courageous and I'm ashamed to say that I was not one of them."

But Schmalz knew he could have a different and larger impact. He was an insider—a skillful writer, extraordinary editor, avid protector of *Times* standards and traditions and masterful office politician—whose career was born and bred at the *Times,* and who was clearly headed for greater things in the paper's power structure. He had attained a level of trust from his editors that few others in a similar situation could possibly match. And he was determined to use his "dual identity," as he called it, to spotlight the challenges, hopes and fears of the community of AIDS sufferers that he inhabited both publicly in the pages of the *Times* and privately among its editors, prodding the latter to improve the paper's coverage as a public policy issue, not just a medical or human interest issue.

"For 20 years, I had been a by-the-book Timesman, no personal involvement allowed," he wrote in an intensely personal account in the *Week in Review* in December 1992, two years after his collapse. "But now I see the world through the prism of AIDS. I feel an obligation to those with AIDS to write about it and an obligation to the newspaper to write what just about no other reporter in America can cover in quite the same way. And I feel an obligation to myself. This is the place—reporting—where I am at home. This is the place where I must come to terms with AIDS."

In the same article, he told of drawing the line between activism and journalism, of feeling out of place at an AIDS funeral after another reporter asked whether he was there as a reporter or a gay man with AIDS. Having responded "reporter" to the dismay of activists, he added: "Some people think it is the journalism that suffers, that objectivity is abandoned. But they are wrong. If the reporters have any integrity at all, it is they who suffer, caught between two allegiances."

AFTER THE ONSET OF THE DISEASE, Schmalz—not previously one to overindulge himself in moments of self-reflection—became less focused on the *Times*, less defined by it, more philosophical. He wrote that his spirituality had increased. He told one group of young students that he had been given "time to get my life in order; my life is more together now than it ever was." Indeed, after years of solo existence, Schmalz began a relationship with a man he met in a support group; after inhabiting a series of spare apartments that served mostly to hold his carefully selected wardrobe and piles of newspapers, he purchased a small penthouse on the upper west side of Manhattan, whether in a quest for comfort, an expression of confidence or an act of denial.

Schmalz's last article was written as his health went into its final decline, and appeared in *The New York Times Magazine* on November 28, 1993, a few weeks after his death on November 6. It reflected an anger and desperation he had withheld from earlier reports. "Once AIDS was a hot topic in America," he wrote, "promising treatments on the horizon, intense media interest, a political battlefield. Now, 12 years after it was first recognized as a new disease, AIDS has become normalized, part of the landscape.

"It is at once everywhere and nowhere, the leading cause of death among young men nationwide, but little threat to the core of American political power, the white heterosexual suburbanite. No cure or vaccine is in sight. And what small treatment advances had been won are now crumbling. The world is moving on, uncaring, frustrated and bored, leaving by the roadside those of us who are infected and who can't help but wonder: Whatever happened to AIDS?"

The words echoed at least as far as the White House, where President Clinton centered his World AIDS Day speech around Schmalz's article, answering his blunt question—"I am dying. Why doesn't someone help us?"—by responding, "I have to say that I think that is a good question and a good challenge." And they reverberated at his memorial service a few weeks later, where grief-struck friends and colleagues, including Sulzberger and Lelyveld, spoke to mark what would have been Schmalz's 40th birthday on December 6.

THESE DAYS, more than six years later, AIDS appears only sporadically as a cause of death in the paper's obituaries. Where sophisticated medical care exists, the advanced, multidrug treatments that came a few years too late for Schmalz are prolonging the lives of many of those who now have AIDS; in the United States, at least, new infections have slowed. The *Times* is covering AIDS developments—advancements and setbacks in treating the disease—and has done a particularly good job of telling the stories of countries where modern care is out of reach. But with the urgency diminished, so too is the frequency. The politics of AIDS and the mechanics of the disease are skillfully described, but the human stories that Schmalz told with such clarity and passion are more rare.

Being gay at the *Times*, meanwhile, has become unremarkable, and being gay in the pages of the *Times* is perhaps even more so. Gay people serve comfortably in the newsroom and the executive ranks. The new *Times* stylebook prefers gay to homosexual, a linguistic turnabout unthinkable 15 years ago when the word gay was largely banned from the paper's pages. There is no longer an individual reporter assigned to cover gay or AIDS issues—a fact that activists lament—but coverage of gay issues is frequent and prominent in the paper, and the lives of gay people appear routinely among the lives of others. As Schmalz asserted, the spark of change may have begun before him. But he knew how to make it burn.

Richard J. Meislin, a friend and colleague of Jeffrey Schmalz's for 18 years, is editor in chief of New York Times Digital, the new media arm of The New York Times Co.

14

Native American Newspapers

Telling Uncomfortable Truths in Tribal Journalism

Mark N. Trahant

I KNOW THE EXACT DAY when I started thinking like a journalist.

In 1977, I had a new job, editor of a tribal newspaper, the *Sho-Ban News,* published on the Shoshone-Bannock Tribe Indian Reservation in Idaho. I was 19 years old and working in what should have been an impossible climate to learn journalism: I was a government employee. My salary came from a federal make-work program, the Comprehensive Employment and Training Act (CETA). My boss was a tribal official, and ultimately we both worked for a political authority, the tribal council. This is not an unusual situation in Indian Country. Most tribal newspapers are divisions of government and editors act as public extensions of tribal councils. Some tribal editors are even charged with a "public relations" role as part of their job description.

But my view of journalism was shaped on February 24, 1977.

Another federal agency, the Bureau of Indian Affairs, hosted a conference on tribal journalism in Spokane, Washington. At one of the sessions, a reporter from a local newspaper offered this advice: "Be a house organ."

"Keep that in mind, always. You must slant everything that you write. . . . You're presenting [news] only from the point of view of your boss," the reporter said. "A paper like this is not to air your dirty linen . . . even your letters to the editor should be reflective of the message you're trying to convey."

But a Yakama tribal member, and journalist, stood up and confronted the speaker. "I have to admit you're making me extremely angry with your presumption about Indian newspapers as 'house organs.' Are you aware of the 1968 law that guarantees freedom of the press in Indian Country?" asked Richard LaCourse. "Indian newspapers should be professional, straight reporting operations, and your presumption about becoming cheerleaders for a point of view has nothing to do with the field of journalism. Why are you making this presumption?"

The reporter tried to dismiss the criticism, joking that "the point of his whole speech was down the drain."

Perhaps for the speaker, but not for me. That moment opened my mind to the potential of tribal journalism.

LaCourse taught me the importance of a voice that serves a community best by telling the truth, even when truth is uncomfortable. It is this commitment that requires courage on the part of a tribal editor. Sometimes you have to publish stories that your bosses would prefer remain hidden away from view. You have to regularly ask yourself what becomes the first question of native journalism: do you work for your readers or for those who are elected to govern a tribal nation?

THIS IS NOT a new dilemma. the first native newspaper was the *Cherokee Phoenix* published on February 27, 1828, in the tribal capital of New Echota, in what is now Georgia. The editor, Elias Boudinot, created what he called a "vehicle of Indian intelligence" and saw freedom as the essential element for the newspaper's discussion on matters of politics, religion and so forth. Of course governments were not keen to support Boudinot's vehicle.

Georgians had been seeking to oust their Cherokee neighbors for decades. The state enacted a number of laws in the 1820s designed to destroy Cherokee sovereignty—and the will of tribal members to resist "removal" from their homeland. Col. C.H. Nelson, of the Georgia Guard, had Boudinot brought before the state militia in a "libel" action. While in custody, Nelson told Boudinot that he could not be prosecuted under Georgia law, but the editor could be tied to a tree and given a sound whipping if he didn't stop attacking state sovereignty.

Boudinot responded with a series of editorials on the Guard and press freedom. "In this free country, where the liberty of the press is solemnly guaranteed, is this the way to obtain satisfaction for an alleged injury committed in a newspaper? I claim nothing . . . of which a privileged white editor would not complain."

Despite a number of legal victories, Boudinot was convinced that the Cherokees would never be allowed to live in peace. He was persuaded that removal was the only option—and this conviction put him in conflict with tribal authorities because even the discussion of removal was considered treasonous under tribal law. The Cherokee Constitution did not guarantee a free press, and tribal leaders argued that the editor, and the newspaper, were merely instruments of public policy.

Boudinot resigned as editor, and not long after his newspaper was destroyed by the Georgia Guard. Cherokee politics was no more forgiving. A few years later Boudinot was murdered, labeled by some as a traitor, for supporting enemies of Cherokee sovereignty.

This tragedy is a legacy, one shared by tribal journalists today. Reporters, editors, broadcasters and storytellers routinely decide how much they're willing to risk before they publish a story or engage in the normal discourse of journalism.

FIVE YEARS AFTER LaCourse awakened me at the *Sho-Ban News* I was asked to edit, and later serve as publisher of, the *Navajo Times*. The Navajo tribe is the largest in the country and in recognition of its sovereignty is often called the Navajo Nation. Altogether, the Navajo Nation is a community of some 200,000 people and a huge land mass that stretches over an area larger than many states. The newspaper in March of 1984 had just become a daily, and reporters and editors were experimenting with our new deadlines—and how we covered our community.

Start with the coverage of a routine election, a normal process for reporters writing about any city, state or nation. But the *Navajo Times* had to figure out how to write about two candidates, one a former tribal chairman and the other the incumbent chairman. The winner of the election would become the paper's next boss. It was like reporters and editors at *The Washington Post* working for the president of the United States.

We tried to ignore tribal government officials and concentrate on a kind of journalism that would serve our readers.

"We wanted to cover the election differently than it ever had been before," recalled Managing Editor Monty Roessel. "We wanted it covered from a Navajo point of view."

The first election story was an announcement of a "Draft Peter MacDonald" campaign. MacDonald had been chairman of the tribe and had been defeated four years earlier by Peterson Zah, then the director of a public interest law firm. The 1986 election was an extraordinary rematch. We assigned reporters who spoke Navajo and tried to cover the election issues in depth. For example, when MacDonald declared his candidacy he said in the Navajo language that the police were harassing bootleggers. He did not repeat that in his English version. But reporter Betty Reid did.

On another occasion, the MacDonald campaign released a picture of the former chairman with President Ronald Reagan. After the meeting, the campaign said Reagan had "reached a new level of understanding" on issues affecting Navajo people. We reported that the "meeting" was a reception line that lasted four or five seconds. The *Times* was told by a White House official: "There was no meeting," and it "put the president in an awkward position because he did not have a discussion of any kind with MacDonald."

On Friday, August 22, 1986, I wrote an editorial calling for a debate between Chairman Peterson Zah and former Chairman Peter MacDonald. The *Times* offered to negotiate between the two sides and act as the sponsor.

"If such a debate is to take place it will certainly be the first, that I recall," wrote council delegate Percy Deal. "I for one look forward to it."

A few months later, the Times rented out Window Rock's movie theater, printed tickets and, on October 21, 1986, hosted the first public debate for chairman of the *Navajo Nation*. The *Times* was covering the news—and making news. The Associated Press was there, The *Arizona Republic*, the *Albuquerque* (N.M.) *Journal*, as well as TV stations from Albuquerque.

THE *TIMES* ALSO FACED the question of endorsements. I met with the reporters and asked them what they thought. Nearly everyone on staff thought we should not endorse any candidate because the Times was owned by the tribe, and an endorsement would make it more difficult for the reporters to cover the campaigns.

I listened. Then I went in my office and shut the door. Without telling anyone (except Monty Roessel because I asked him to edit the piece), I wrote the editorial endorsing Peterson Zah for re-election. I felt strongly that the newspaper ought to take a stand for one reason— Zah believed, and lived up to, the notion of a free press.

Zah never acted like a newspaper's boss. Our editorials championed the enactment of a tribal ethics law (at first opposed by many tribal council members), and we pointed out when the Zah administration failed to live up to its promises. We also covered the Navajo-Hopi land dispute, an intense, complicated issue, without becoming cheerleaders for the Navajo government (our readership included the Hopi Reservation as well).

I know our criticism was seen as an act of betrayal by some Zah supporters. They wanted the newspaper to be on the team. But because the newspaper had the freedom to report unpleasant things, I thought we should take the next step and endorse the chairman for re-election.

The next morning several reporters were furious—they were uncomfortable with the *Times'* editorial. I told them they could honestly say they did not know anything about it. Roessel left a sealed note on my desk that said, "Mark: The more I thought about today's edit, the clearer it became that this was the only thing we could do and still be true to our beliefs. In my view, printing the edit is one of the most courageous things you have done for this paper. Sometimes it takes guts to be right—as you proved today. Monty."

Of course all of this is routine at most newspapers, but Indian Country is different. Indeed, two reporters wrote about how difficult this whole election business was at the *Navajo Times*. When Betty Reid reported that the speech MacDonald gave in the Navajo language he never would have said in English because he defended bootleggers selling alcohol in a remote community, the campaign complained. It said the reporter picked out sensational quotes that somehow did not translate well into English. "I'm fully bilingual and am not ashamed of my beautiful Navajo accent," Reid wrote. "But what those lawyers never understood is Mr. MacDonald's skillful use of the Navajo language. He's able to bring humor to an issue while at the same time effectively pushing the issue. He makes people listen and laugh."

LeNora Begay also wrote about the difficulty of covering a tribal election. "My own relatives questioned where my loyalties lay. And to be perfectly honest, I sometimes didn't know," she wrote. "It hurts to be in the middle of what has become a dirty campaign. Yet I know it is a feeling shared by most of the reporters on the newspaper. It was as if because I was Navajo, Navajo readers did not trust me. I became labeled a Zah supporter or a MacDonald supporter and not as a journalist."

OUR HEADLINE THE DAY after the election read: CLIFFHANGER: IT'S MACDONALD. When the final numbers were reported, Peter MacDonald had been returned to his old post by less than 1 percent of the vote.

Since I was publisher, and had endorsed the losing candidate, I figured I was certain to be fired. I even set out to make the first move, calling for an appointment with the chairman-elect. I briefed MacDonald on our financial situation (we were losing money) and offered my resignation. I will never forget what happened next: MacDonald put his arm around me, said he respected my work and did not want me to go. He said he would be in touch about future changes. Perhaps it was election euphoria. I don't know.

The *Navajo Times* kept at it. Our coverage of the inauguration was first-rate. We published a special section, with seven stories on nearly every angle and a complete text of MacDonald's inaugural remarks. But we also continued on our independent course.

The Times questioned the cost of MacDonald's inauguration—a lavish ceremony and party—as well as the administration's hiring of a new Washington public relations firm. Our editorial policy supported an active government-jobs creation program, and we were disappointed when that election promise didn't seem to move anywhere after the inauguration. When the MacDonald administration failed to quickly fill an important post, we wrote:

"Good Morning. It's now the 9th day of February. It's the 28th day of the MacDonald administration," said one editorial. "The days, the numbers, are important because the Navajo Nation still does not have a director for its economic development division. ..." Clearly, the *Navajo Times* was going to chronicle the MacDonald administration—good and bad.

As a tribal employee, a manager, I kept the tribe informed about our financial progress. We had spent nearly $1.4 million converting to a daily, and it would have taken us another four or five years to break even. Moreover, the paper did not have a legal charter, we had a tax problem left over from a previous administration, and we still needed capital for expansion.

But I was so confident about the future that I arranged to meet with the *Mesa* (Ariz.) *Tribune* to possibly buy a used computer from their circulation department. On Thursday morning, February 19, 1987, I called the tribal administration to see if they had any additional ideas about a memorandum I had sent. I asked if they wanted to meet. "No. Not today," I was told. So I went to Mesa.

Then a rumor started: the *Times* was to be closed. A few hours after I left town, a few *Times* reporters' spotted the chairman at a hotel and asked him what was going on. MacDonald said the administration had decided to close the *Times*.

Reporters and editors geared up for a final edition. "We made assignments. Reporters were making calls, interviewing people on the street about their reaction," said Roessel. "I wanted everyone to write their own obit."

But a few minutes after the chance encounter with MacDonald, tribal police were dispatched to the newspaper. There, they handed out copies of the closure order. Employees were given three weeks of severance pay and the "reasonable time" of 15 minutes to get their personal belongings out of the building.

Police sealed the building, taped its front door and labeled it "evidence." (Roessel and I were specifically banned from the building. But Monty was quick-thinking and packed up my files into photo boxes and took them to the safety of his car.)

The daily newspaper that had broken so many Navajo stories could not write its own obituary—that had to be left to public statements from MacDonald and later from the scores of regional and national publications covering our demise.

"The *Times* is a runaway drain on our general funds, an uncontrolled hemorrhaging either ignored or tacitly condoned by the prior administration," a MacDonald statement said. "As these facts were brought to my attention by my accounting and legal counsel, I had no choice . . . but to order the newspaper's operations suspended."

MacDonald's contention that we would lose $1 million that year was essentially correct—especially when you add in the costs of closing the newspaper down (perhaps it even went higher). But those who wanted the press stilled ignored other numbers. For example the *Times'* circulation had grown from a little more than 2,000 copies a day to more than 7,000 a day (including a 32 percent increase from February 1986 to the same month a year later). We had some days of the week that were profitable (nearly every Friday edition made money—many had more than 50 pages with 60 percent advertising). And, we were getting stronger every week. Several of us had even offered to buy the *Times*—an offer that was never discussed.

But MacDonald did not sell the newspaper because a "real" newspaper was not in his interest. The newspaper was closed for a time and then reopened as a noncontroversial, official tribal publication.

But this too is an old story in tribal journalism.

ONLY A DECADE LATER another editor of the *Navajo Times*, now published as a weekly, had another confrontation with tribal leaders. In March 1997, reporter Marley Shebala sent out an e-mail warning that her editor, Tom Arviso Jr., might soon be fired for writing about the tribal administration. Tribal journalists rallied to support Arviso. He kept his job and went on to win an award from the Native American Journalists Association for his courage.

The same story could be told about Dan Agent, editor of the *Cherokee Advocate*. The nation's second largest tribe operated with the editor acting as director of public relations—making it even more difficult for the editor to defy the party line. But in 1997 the newspaper attempted to write straight news accounts of a power struggle between Cherokee Principal Chief Joe Byrd and his political opponents. Byrd's administration responded by "restructuring" the newspaper, firing all but a clerk-typist and hiring an editor who would write the party line. Four years later, after Byrd's defeat at the polls, Agent is once again running the Advocate.

This same kind of story could be told for a Pueblo journalist who said something unkind—and a week later lost the *Pueblo News'* entire budget. Lori Edmo-Suppah, editor of the *Sho-Ban News*, and president of NAJA in 2000, wrote that tribal newspapers ought to be the voice of the people. "I still believe this, despite attempts by tribal politicians . . . to manipulate the tribal press into printing only what they want tribal citizens to know.

"I've learned that it takes courage to seek the truth, and the journalistic integrity to print the truth when doing so might cost your job."

Edmo-Suppah was ordered not to print a story about tribal budget cuts in 1994. She complied with the order—and then wrote an editorial about how misguided the council's decision was. The tribal council threatened to cut the newspaper's budget too—but tribal members came to the paper's defense saying the *Sho-Ban News* was a community asset.

Edmo-Suppah's story is not about any one journalist's courage. It's about every tribal journalist who has to balance the cause of truth with community politics and everyone who believes in discourse as the best way to inform a community.

Indian Country swings back and forth between community dialogue and tribal council control, but it doesn't have to be that way. Native American communities have a rich history of discourse—even when the truth expressed makes us uncomfortable. It is this heritage that keeps the best Native American journalists going, knowing that they provide tribal members with solid information and discussion. It's a way of working directly for their people, their readers.

Tribal leaders are mistaken when they close down discussion. They make a community weaker, not stronger. The cause of truth is the cause of Indian Country.

Mark N. Trahant is a columnist at the Seattle Times *and a member of the Shoshone-Bannock tribe of Idaho.*

15

Breaking Ranks in Northern Ireland

Hard Questions and Dangerous Silences

Malachi O'Doherty

NORTHERN IRELAND HAS SERVED as a nursery slope war for many journalists who went on to cover strife in Beirut, South Africa and Kosovo. It has been suited to this because it is safer and has always been safer than those other places at their worst.

For most of the Troubles, up to the cease-fire of 1994, violence came in a steady drip that never produced more than 100 deaths a year in a region with a population of 1.5 million. Most of the likely targets knew who they were: police officers on patrol, soldiers guarding them, political activists, construction workers repairing bombed police stations, taxi drivers, anyone related to any of these categories who might share in the blast of an undercar bomb or take a ricochet, and random Catholics, or Protestants mistaken for Catholics, who might wander into a dangerous area or whose work might make them accessible. That's what explains the targeting of taxi drivers. Then there were the people caught in explosions, over and over again, at La Mon House, Enniskillen, Claudy. These were the random victims. Any of us could have been among them, the journalist as much as the clergyperson.

I remember a colleague joking with me back in 1972, the worst year of the violence. He said: "I hear Don McCullen is in town. Things must be getting really serious."

McCullen had made his reputation with his Vietnam pictures. The joke, recalling it now, tells me that even then our primary concern was that things would get worse. We could live with the violence as it was, but our dread was that a greater calamity was imminent. If McCullen preferred to be in Belfast, did that mean that he thought Belfast was more fearsome than Saigon? If so, then bigger fool him. Often during the worst violence, Belfast people felt the whole world was bored with them. They read intense news interest as a form of respect. That is what they felt when Kate Adie, the international BBC television reporter, arrived to cover street rioting in the mid-'90s. It indicated that the world was paying attention to us again after decades of bewilderment and disdain.

This is not to say that Northern Ireland hasn't had its hairy moments.

"Do you know, you look a bit like Jim Campbell," said a man in the headquarters building of the Loyalist—that is to say Protestant—Ulster Defence Association, when I went there to interview their leaders in the early 1980s. I did know I looked like Campbell because I had worked with him, perhaps even modeled myself a bit on him. The man drew a large folding knife from his pocket and raised it to my beard.

"With a wee bit off there and a wee bit off there, you'd look just like him."

Humor? I wasn't laughing.

Jim Campbell was the one journalist to be shot in Belfast. A loyalist, representing a different group, the Ulster Volunteer Force, shot him at his front door one evening because he had been writing about a UVF man shortly to be released from prison.

Jim survived the shooting.

"We sometimes drive past his house and give him a wee wave, just to see him shit himself," said the man with the knife.

THERE IS A PROTOCOL, accepted by those we have taken for the most crazed demons on earth, that a journalist, even from an enemy country, is due some immunity not extended to ordinary citizens and is exempted from the vague, ever-changing lists of supposed legitimate targets. In Northern Ireland, the Republican paramilitaries learned this protocol before the Loyalists did.

I very much doubt that Sinn Féin, the political party representing the interests of the Provisional IRA, would scare a journalist in their own offices like that. They have a better sense of public relations, always have. They also have a political need to define themselves as the businesslike diplomatic Republicans who can mediate with the passions of the IRA and their support community. Officials of Sinn Féin may be the same men who stalked with guns, plotted bombings or rose to political influence through murder and sabotage—but they recoil as coyly from the suggestion of this as any prim lady from a smutty joke. They train us, by their manner, not to even think about the blood on their hands, let alone to ask about it.

Go ahead and ask anyway, and they get very angry.

A former IRA man called Bobby Storey was described by Liam Clarke in the *Sunday Times* as the man whose job it was to police the IRA cease-fire. I knew little about him. I had read Kevin Toolis' book, *Rebel Hearts*, and his interview with Dermot Finucane, describing how ruthlessly he and Storey would take over a family house for an attack. I had read J. Bowyer Bell's account of how Storey acquired the nickname Brain Surgeon for shooting people in the head. I wrote a commentary for the BBC Radio Ulster program "Talkback" about the integrity of the peace process, saying, "We are dependent on this man now, all of us. How do we feel about that?"

This was a question about the integrity of the process. Storey took my point personally. Perhaps he felt that the nickname Brain Surgeon implied sarcastically that he was stupid. In Belfast humor that is most likely what it would mean. He took me into the corner of a bar and explained that I was a slug. He's about twice the size of me. I listened with care. You don't argue in those situations. If such a man invites you to consider that you are worthless and contemptible, then that's what you apply your mind to, because intimidation works—it makes us timid.

Journalism, however, especially the journalism of the columnist and the book writer, allows you the last word, or at least a reply. I wrote up the incident as the introduction to my book, *The Trouble With Guns,* as much to manage the fright I had taken as to illustrate the moral complexities of the peace process.

When a colleague asked Storey why he had leaned on me, Storey said I should not presume to go into bars in Republican areas just because I grew up there and then feel free to criticize Republicans in my writing. There was a price to be paid for disagreeing, and that was that you kept your distance.

IT IS GETTING EASIER FOR people in Republican areas to express dissent, though most of this comes from people who "have backings"—former members of the IRA themselves, or of other Republican groups like the Official IRA. These people cannot be attacked without some risk of bloody and sudden retaliation.

For others it is different. I have often sat in the homes of people who are furious with the IRA, particularly because of the behavior of their vigilantes who supervise the behavior of young people and punish with leg breakings and gunshot woundings. They say to me, "Of course, around here you keep your head down and say nothing."

Belfast is a small city, with a population of under half a million, but the people who live there tend not to move outside their own areas much. The west of the city, around the mainly Catholic Falls Road, is almost like a separate town. Many who live there would not contemplate living elsewhere; they would regard it as a risk to live close to Protestants. The boundaries between politically intense Republican or Loyalist communities and the neutral areas are often precise, and the remove one would have to make to get out of one might only be half a mile, even 100 yards.

An indicator of the call of communal allegiance is that people declare themselves Catholic and Protestant without meaning anything theological at all. The Protestant may be an atheist; the Catholic may believe in reincarnation. The clinging to labels is a symptom of their need to belong in separate camps and tells nothing specific about the body of beliefs they actually hold. In such a society it is very difficult for anyone to stand out and say, "Well actually, none of this applies to me."

My freedom of expression was gained by moving three miles from where I grew up at the top of Belfast Falls Road. That has always been the main artery road of Catholic west Belfast. I went from there to live in a mixed area near Queen's University, where a more normal civic polity applies. I have created a space for myself from which I can state bluntly, as an analyst and commentator, what I think are the flaws in the culture of Irish Nationalism.

I had already mentally left a Catholic and chauvinistic education behind before the Troubles started with a feeling like being released from prison. I had supported the first stirrings of a civil rights campaign precisely because it was making demands on the state without asserting an ethnic claim; it was about reforming the state, not over-throwing it. After 50 years of partition, most Catholics had accepted that the old argument was obsolete; the problem was how to find a secure place for Catholics within Northern Ireland, not how to topple Protestants into a united Ireland and replicate the problem of division with Catholics on top.

That is still how most Catholics think. I am not in a minority position.

In some ways I was as conservative as the Republican traditional-ists who had assimilated from their parents as children the conviction that they had inherited an unfinished war.

I HAD BEEN A REPUBLICAN at 13, but my mother scoffed at me reading braggardly accounts of guerrilla war in 1919. The old arguments about Irish identity and British oppression had divided generations of Catho-lic families, aside from what they had done to separate Catholic from Protestant. Other mothers were proud of sons who tended towards revolution. They shut their eyes to the damage they were doing and fantasized that they were fighting a war when they were blowing up shops, and often themselves, and shooting policemen and endangering the people they presumed to defend. I—when I got over the first trauma of what was happening—saw nothing more worthwhile to do than to question their mythologies and their self-delusions, though that response might have been a product of upbringing too.

I have drawn criticism.

One of the core ideas of working-class politics, promoted by both Loyalist and Republican paramilitaries, is the need for community cohesion and solidarity around the cause. The paramilitary organiza-tions on both sides have tried to monopolize the expression of the areas they occupy. Contradict them and you are not just a traitor to a political cause, you are a defector from your own root community.

It needles dangerous people at their most sensitive point when some-one with roots in their community dissents assertively from what they say is the community experience. They argue that there is a higher form of democracy than electoral politics, the democracy of the community's voice. The community, as they presume to define it, is what has rights of expression—not the individual. The individual's divergent point of view is dangerous if it dilutes the community's coherence and thereby undermines the political cause of Republican or Loyalist parties. In a profoundly divided society like Northern Ireland, a failure of community allegiance can be read as succor to the enemy.

A person who was raised as a Catholic and a Nationalist who attacks the IRA for unwarranted murder or criticizes their political proxies for dishonesty will be accused by some of being a traitor. I have been accused of sanctioning the loyalist murder of Republicans, and not just in whining letters to the editor but from the platform of a political party conference, while I was actually sitting at the press desk below the speaker, who was a convicted terrorist.

The background to that incident was the murder of Malachy Carey. He was a Sinn Féin party worker, and he had been shot dead on his doorstep by Loyalists. Sinn Féin blamed the media for jeopardizing their members by "demonizing" them. What the media had been doing was drawing attention to the fact that Republicans were the more aggressive terrorist faction and questioning the right of their political representatives to present an image of themselves merely as victims.

But the moral power of their blaming the media was fearsome. What journalist wants to be held complicit in murder? The political device of Sinn Féin, which baffled nearly every interviewer, was the insistence that the IRA and Sinn Féin be regarded as wholly separate, regardless of the fact that they shared membership on all levels, including at the very top of both.

Journalists who tried to penetrate that conceit were being told that they had blood on their hands, though it is absurd to imagine that Loyalist killers—who were content to kill any Catholics—were in need of journalists to connect Sinn Féin to the IRA before they would select a target.

I wanted to refuse the assumption that because I had an Irish name and had been raised in a Catholic family with Nationalist politics, that I was cast that way for life. I had a right to think my way through to a different position.

THE DIVISION OF SOCIETY IN Northern Ireland is all pervasive, and there is no real escape available, even for those who insist on independent thinking.

There is another community typecasting you, apart from your own, and you can have no control over what people there think of you. You can feel implicated by their anger. When a Protestant Unionist attacks the IRA, it is embarrassing to agree. You feel that that anger really addresses all Catholics, including yourself, and you react defensively, or you genuinely feel that you know better than the angry Protestant what makes someone join the IRA, and that you can't fairly align yourself with simplistic hurt and bitterness.

Because the conflict is seen as ethnic, broadcasters and newspapers tend to seek balance by selecting interviewees and commentators according to their perceived ethnic background, rather than according to their actual political positions. I get invited as a commentator frequently onto television and radio programs, and routinely I am matched against a Protestant, on the understanding that that provides a simple, both sides of the house equation, even though we may actually agree. Perceived Catholic/Nationalists like me, therefore, when matched against actual Protestant/Unionists will upset the actual balance of discussion if they break from expectation and argue against a home position.

Local newspapers try to field an equal number of Catholic and Protestant columnists. It doesn't matter that they might agree, the difference in their roots will satisfy for ethnic balance, and that is what is seen to matter most. Yet, with this conscientious pairing, when one has crossed over, the betrayal is seen as even greater, because it deprives one side of any airing at all in that debate.

As someone who grew up in a Northern Irish Catholic home, in a Northern Irish Catholic area, I am perceived as letting the side down by joining these debates. A sense of community allegiance should oblige me to make the Nationalist case or let a real Nationalist take my place.

NORTHERN IRELAND'S COMPLEXITIES demand fair assessment, but sometimes the best journalistic response to the repetitive ideological intransigence of politicians who sustain division is the unanswerable question that penetrates hypocrisy. In August 1999, Dr. Mo Mowlam, then Northern Ireland Secretary of State, was agonizing over whether the IRA, by murdering Charles Bennet, a young Catholic, had broken its cease-fire and drawn political exclusion on its proxy party, Sinn Féin. The appalling anomaly appeared to be that paramilitaries might be above all political sanction for murder, so long as Catholics only killed Catholics and Protestants only killed Protestants.

I asked Sinn Féin's chief negotiator Martin McGuinness at a press conference, with no expectation of an answer: "Martin, if you shot me, would that be a breach of the cease-fire." The other reporters fell about laughing. The point was made that the usual evasions were not taken seriously, even if they were always taken down and reported.

The irony of my position when I criticized Republicans in Sinn Féin and the IRA was that I simply compounded the danger for me that most people face already. As far as Loyalist thugs were concerned, I was still a taig, an Irish Catholic, and their ethnic enemy: I could no more have denied that to them than I could have insisted on not being male or white. At least if I had known my place as a taig I would only have had one set of angry men to worry about, the enemy that I had inherited as a Catholic—the Protestants. In terms of personal security, it made little sense to double the number of dangerous people who might be annoyed with me.

Yet my somewhat anomalous stance has its value because it expresses publicly the anger of many others who feel silenced not just by fear of the other side, but also by the protocol of the peace process itself. Nonviolent Nationalists who support the Social Democratic and Labour Party will defend Sinn Féin against Unionist criticism. That is what they feel they must do to preserve Republican involvement in the peace process. At the same time, they are embarrassed by Republican brutality.

The opinions that people air in private are, according to common lore, more pro-violent than those they air in public. In fact, for many it works the other way around. A lot of people in Northern Ireland are more accommodating in private and more considerate of the enemy's point of view than they publicly acknowledge. They like it when someone like me stands up and excoriates paramilitary organizations. Their politicians, who are maintaining a diplomatic relationship with Sinn Féin, for instance, and hold their anger in check and risk appearing to take a soft line on violence, may be heartened to hear a journalist, tied to no party affiliation, scalding the very people they have to be nice to.

At the start of the peace process, journalists debated whether they should help it by confirming its orthodoxies, for instance, that conflict had been an inevitable product of the past. Some of us fretted whether, in challenging those orthodoxies and picking apart the spurious political argument of violent people new to politics, we might not be driving them back to violence. Most people want the peace process to work, but they want a process that is durable enough to withstand common logic.

People tell me that ordinary reportage and interviewing have failed them, that they have failed to cut through the conceits and the piety, that passionate commentary serves them better. In a frightened society, they tell me that quietly—but they tell me it often.

Malachi O'Doherty, a free-lance journalist in Belfast, Northern Ireland, writes political commentaries for The Belfast Telegraph, The Scotsman *and the BBC. He is author of* The Trouble With Guns: Republican Strategy *and* The Provisional IRA.

16

Church and State

Finding the Courage to Maintain Integrity

Leo Bogart

IN 1920, THE RADICAL WRITER Upton Sinclair compared American journalistic practice to the "brass check" by which whorehouse clients selected their partners. In that era, proprietors of coal mines, railways and steel mills owned many newspapers and bribed others to advance their interests. Sinclair thought the press of his day was in the pocket of vested industrial interests, not only because they were big advertisers but because they held financial and political power in their home communities.

Today the nonjournalistic business considerations that enter into management's judgments on critical issues are more diverse and infinitely more powerful. They entail relations with government, with advertisers, with audiences and with elements in the media organization itself. Balancing the resulting cross pressures often requires difficult, painful and courageous ethical decisions.

American reporters have faced the threat of jail when they have refused to reveal confidential sources, but they are rarely forced to exhibit physical courage of the kind required by their counterparts in countries like Colombia or Algeria, where newspeople are murdered routinely. Examples of courage are harder to find when it carries less severe penalties. In recent times, two investigative reporters, the *Arizona Republic*'s Don Bolles, Manuel de Dios Unanue of New York's

El Diario/La Prensa, have been murdered as a result of their reporting on organized crime—but such instances of vengeance are rare.

The most often mentioned illustrations of journalistic courage involve the people at the top of organizations that have uncovered news that endangers the health or even the survival of the enterprise. Few such instances are widely publicized, perhaps because courage is manifested routinely in publishers' support of their newsrooms' investigations.

Consider the most frequently cited cases: Edward R. Murrow's exposé of Sen. Joseph McCarthy (according to Murrow, CBS management's reaction was, "Good show. Sorry you did it," but they stuck by him), Carl Bernstein and Bob Woodward's investigation of the Watergate break-in, Seymour Hersh's revelation of the My Lai massacre, *The New York Times'* publication of the Pentagon Papers. All of them involved intrepid and resourceful reporting of buried information that presented a threat to powerful political figures or institutions. But all also required the support of media chief executives who weighed their civic responsibility against their enterprises' material interests. (President Nixon wanted to divest the Washington Post Co. of its valuable television franchises.)

The process of balancing journalistic and business imperatives is never simple when it involves the public's right to know deadly national secrets. President Roosevelt tried to press treason charges against the *Chicago Tribune*'s Robert McCormick when he published a story that revealed to the Japanese (though they apparently did not understand it) that the U.S. had broken their naval code. In contrast, Orville Dryfoos, the publisher of *The New York Times*, withheld an already published report of the CIA's preparations for the Bay of Pigs invasion because he thought this would not be in the national interest. He later regretted his decision. Similarly, the NBC Nightly News killed a report on U.S. satellite spying when Secretary of Defense Casper Weinberger called to say it would endanger the lives of American agents. The story turned up in *The Washington Post* two days later. The Pentagon's public relations arm wanted the story kept secret so that it could be released on its own timetable, to demonstrate the military's technical achievement.

Warren Christopher, when Undersecretary of State in 1980, at the behest of the Saudi ambassador, asked the Public Broadcasting Service to withhold the airing of a British documentary, "The Death of a

Princess," on the grounds that it might provoke a new oil crisis. At PBS Lawrence Grossman held firm, and there were no repercussions.

As TECHNOLOGY BLURS the distinction between print and electronics, the success of media businesses depends increasingly on the decisions of government, embodied in regulations, legislation and judicial rulings. This must make the people who run them more sensitive to the political effects of their news coverage. As political advertising has become a considerable component of television revenues, politicians have found it increasingly necessary and expedient to court the media, creating a new source of pressure on journalists.

Media overlords rarely give direct orders to kill or slant stories. They do not have to do that in order to let it be known what their views are and where their interests lie. They hire and fire editors and producers. Almost imperceptible Pavlovian cues reinforce desired behavior and inhibit what is unwelcome.

The head of an individually or family-owned media business may be more willing to take risks than the chief executive of a publicly held company worried about the reaction from Wall Street. But in today's corporate economy, editorial independence does not always jibe with the demands of the bottom line. Following the general trend in American business, media companies have merged into larger and larger organizations, including many with operations outside the media business. The very size of these companies makes their managements less vulnerable to the kinds of advertising pressures that beset smaller media organizations. But it also gives them a large stake in the status quo and broadens the possibilities for conflicts of interest, as in NBC's ownership by General Electric, a huge defense contractor, and Liberty Media's links to AT&T, with its dependence on the favors of legislators and government regulators. Even giants who vigorously compete in some spheres of activity enter easily into joint ventures, thereby extending the boundaries of their corporate interests. In 1998, ABC News discarded an investigative report that raised embarrassing questions about hiring and safety practices at Disney World. ABC News and Disney World are, of course, owned by the same company.

In 1995, CBS's "60 Minutes" dropped an interview with a disaffected executive of Brown & Williamson Tobacco Corp. who accused the company of manipulating nicotine levels in cigarettes in order to maximize their addictive effect. When the story came out, the network's defense was that it faced the serious threat of a libel suit. CBS's then principal owner, Laurence Tisch, was also the main stockholder of Lorillard, another tobacco company. The RJR Nabisco and Philip Morris companies, which own huge food and beverage businesses, are among the largest television advertisers. It is clearly impossible to determine what considerations entered the minds of the CBS executives who decided to kill the interview. It was ultimately broadcast, long after the episode had received widespread attention, but it strains credibility to suggest that there were not other factors in their thinking besides the threat of a lawsuit. The story was well covered by the trade press at the time, thus providing support for the notion that legitimate news cannot be suppressed in a competitive media environment. It was brought to even wider public attention in somewhat embellished form by the 1999 film *The Insider*.

Corporate interests have become ever more global in scope and therefore more sensitive to pressures from the state apparatus of countries where the owners of American media companies do business. When a Singapore court imposed a heavy punitive fine on the *International Herald Tribune* for printing an article on government nepotism, the paper accepted the judgment with the knowledge and consent of its owners, the New York Times Co. and the Washington Post Co. There was a powerful pragmatic reason to do so: it could not otherwise continue to print at that strategically crucial location.

News Corp.'s Rupert Murdoch, who sought to bring pay television to China through his satellite Star TV system, invested heavily in a joint venture with the official People's Daily. He removed BBC World News from Star TV after China complained about its objective coverage. His book publishing house, HarperCollins, published a laudatory biography of Deng Xiaoping by Deng's daughter but canceled HarperCollins' contract to publish the memoirs of Chris Patten, Hong Kong's last British governor and a strong critic of the Communists. The editor of the publishing house was suspended and gagged. These scandalous actions created a sensation in the British press, except in Murdoch's *Times*, where it went unreported for a week.

THE CONFLICT BETWEEN the editorial and business sides is still often thought of in terms of stark and brutal impositions of power, prompted by venality, political ambition, personal friendship or idiosyncrasy: a

publisher suppressing a scandalous news story about a major advertiser, planting a puff piece for another, demanding slanted coverage of
an electoral contest, insisting on publicity for a favorite charity or
actress. Episodes of this kind still happen but, with a few egregious
exceptions, the American press in recent years has generally sought to
report news without conscious bias, regardless of the opinions expressed on the editorial page.

This principle has become more widely followed because of the
attrition in the number of competitive newspapers, diminishing the
partisanship that once characterized the press. Monopoly newspapers
necessarily must be cautious in avoiding offense to any segment of
their audience: they consider their entire market their constituency,
and readers and advertisers always have alternatives to the newspaper.

Although this prompts them to be objective in their reporting, it
may also encourage them to shape their content by marketing criteria
rather than by editorial judgments. There has been widespread acceptance of the notion that the press is just another consumer product and
that success comes from giving the customers "what they want."

As a result, hard news has a diminished presence. Straight news
stories fell from 52 percent of major news media content in 1977 to 32
percent in 1997, while gossip, scandal, celebrity and other "human
interest" stories rose from 15 percent to 43 percent, according to a
study of leading newspapers, the three major network TV newscasts
and newsmagazines *Time* and *Newsweek*. The study, conducted by
The Project for Excellence in Journalism and the Medill News Service, found that the emphasis was on "news you can use." TV magazines primarily featuring lifestyle stories have replaced documentaries.

In television news, the race for ratings has always been the pre-
eminent factor in editorial judgments. Television news has long been
an element in the flow of entertainment, packaged to attract maximum
audiences. Network and station managements have rarely come from
the news side, and the traditional journalistic values have meant little
to them. GE's president, Jack Welch, proposed that the network NBC,
which GE owns, exact a charge from publishers whose authors were
interviewed on the "Today" show. On local newscasts, which get the
bulk of the news viewing, producers are mainly preoccupied with the
attractiveness of the news readers, their costumes and background
sets.

The cosmetics draw attention because they appear to affect the audience ratings, which are important only because news media are economically dependent on advertisers. And from the advertisers' standpoint, it seems perfectly reasonable to avoid positioning sales messages next to objectionable content. (Airline ads are routinely pulled from newspapers when planes crash.) A 1998 survey of advertisers, conducted by the American Association of Advertising Agencies, found that 94 percent "want to be notified in advance of any potentially controversial editorial or program content."

But how far can the avoidance of counterproductive juxtapositions go before it becomes censorious or punitive? "We vote with our dollars," said an automobile dealer displeased with a Minneapolis radio station's consumer report. Chrysler required that magazines carrying its ads notify it in advance "of any editorial content that encompasses sexual, political, social issues or any editorial that might be construed as provocative or offensive." *Esquire* magazine, anticipating Chrysler's reactions, cut a short story with a homosexual theme. The resulting publicity led to a flood of protests and to the resignation of the fiction editor. Chrysler eventually withdrew its requirement. Ford dropped its advertising in *The New Yorker* for six months after obscene rap lyrics were quoted in an article adjacent to one of its ads. IBM withdrew its advertising from *Fortune* after the magazine ran an unflattering article about its chairman and CEO. Cosmopolitan was censured by the American Society of Magazine Editors for running ads for a cosmetics line next to an article dealing with the same branded products.

Of 60 publishers surveyed by *Editor & Publisher* in 1999, virtually all could cite instances where an advertiser had pulled advertising or threatened to do so because of a complaint with the paper's news coverage. One publisher in five said that a newspaper might sometimes consider altering a negative story that affected an advertiser, but nine in 10 said their own papers had never done so.

It takes courage not only to maintain editorial integrity but to adhere to an editorial vision. Media are not only reluctant to offend advertisers; they shape their content to please them. Magazines and cable channels are established to appeal to particular segments of the public that are thought to have value as niche marketing targets; their content is directed to those interests that serve advertisers' purposes.

The purpose of journalism is to disseminate information and ideas. The purpose of marketing is to maximize revenues, which may be done by creating ancillary products that provide new uses for existing assets—as when newspapers set up Web sites or publish books based on articles and photographs in their archives—or by creating new editorial sections that are designed to attract extra advertising whether they deal with a county fair, mutual funds or fall fashions. There has been an explosion in the number of such sections, often created by the paper's advertising department or turned over to an independent contractor who sells the advertising and provides the text.

In magazines and more recently in newspapers, "advertorials" carry not only display advertisements but especially prepared text supporting the advertisers' messages; though labeled as advertising, they are easily mistaken for an integral part of the editorial product. It has even been proposed that advertisers be allowed to "sponsor" certain standing features of a newspaper, like the weather report or baseball box scores, much as they can sponsor a radio or television broadcast.

In films and television shows, product placement blurs the distinction between commercial and noncommercial elements. Brand names and logotypes intrude into strategic positions in sports arenas and adorn the names of stadiums and theaters. On the Internet, colorful and cleverly designed banner ads become almost indistinguishable from the surrounding texts and icons. Even *The New York Times Book Review* list of best sellers carries a link to the Barnes & Noble Web site. Former Surgeon General C. Everett Koop attracted criticism when it was revealed that his Web site, ostensibly a source of authoritative health information, plugged a service in which he had a financial interest.

Is the modification of a newspaper's mix of contents to serve the marketing objective of increased readership qualitatively different from the creation of editorial sections that serve the marketing objective of bringing in increased advertising? Where is the line to be drawn between such sections and those that have long been run on automobiles and real estate or that once made newspaper food pages an outlet for manufacturers' publicity releases?

WHAT IS THE PROPER relationship between a news organization's news and business functions?

The old question became newsworthy late in 1999, after a fierce reaction to a special issue of the *Los Angeles Times' Sunday Magazine* devoted to the just-completed Staples Sports Center. Advertising profits were to be split with the Center, which is a subject of continuing news coverage. Former publisher Otis Chandler, who had built the *Times* into one of the world's great newspapers, said its editorial department had been "abused and misused." The *Times'* new publisher, Kathryn M. Downing, apologized, and the paper ran a brilliant and extensive dissection of the episode by its media reporter, David Shaw. A few months later, the Chandler family sold Times-Mirror to the Tribune Co., and both Downing and Editor Michael Parks left the scene.

Newspaper publishers and editors reacted to the original story in strikingly different ways. Half the publishers surveyed by *Editor & Publisher* considered the Staples Center deal "acceptable." This view was shared by only one-fifth of the 105 editors who responded. Seven out of 10 editors say they should have ultimate authority on editorial decisions; eight out of 10 publishers claim that right.

A third of the publishers report that their papers have had promotional tie-ins or revenue-sharing arrangements with people or institutions they cover in the news. More than half believe that newspapers should publish special sections to obtain more advertising even if the subject is of little reader interest. This is misleading; even a small special interest group of readers may represent a valuable advertising target.

EDITORIAL INDEPENDENCE CAN best be maintained when readers contribute significantly to the cash flow and when advertisers are many and diverse. In today's media environment, these conditions can no longer be taken for granted. As the Internet reshapes mass communication, established media are hard-pressed to maintain their competitive positions and fulfill their traditional functions. They must cut costs and scramble for income in order to survive.

Corporate and agency consolidations make all major media dependent on a reduced number of decision-makers who produce an ever larger share of total ad billings. Publications that formerly relied on readers to provide a substantial part of their revenues, and thus cushioned themselves against advertising pressures, have become increasingly dependent on advertising. The business press now relies largely on free ("controlled") distribution; three-quarters of weekly newspaper circulation is free. Circulation has fallen steadily as a percentage of daily newspaper revenues, from 24 percent in 1992 to 19 percent in 1999.

The "wall" separating editorial departments from contamination was erected well over a century ago when advertising replaced circulation as the mainstay of newspaper revenue. In 1977, a nationwide effort, the Newspaper Readership Project, sought to breach the editorial-business wall by making editors part of a problem-solving team effort to stop the decline of circulation. In newspapers across North America, readership or marketing committees were set up that brought editors together with circulation, promotion and advertising executives. They were encouraged to start with research that provided the information they needed to produce papers that were responsive to readers' characteristics, interests and wishes.

Editors took to this process with varying degrees of enthusiasm, but today they generally understand that their own independence depends on the financial health of the enterprise and that newsroom staffs ought to be aware of this simple truth. They realize that people on the business side aren't all dummies and that success comes easier when all departments communicate and work together. As part of this process, the business side may sometimes have to be reminded that what really sells advertising, in any medium, is the public's respect for its integrity. To maintain that integrity often demands a look beyond the quarterly earnings report. And that takes courage.

Leo Bogart, a 1989–90 Media Studies Center fellow, is the former executive vice president and general manager of the Newspaper Advertising Bureau. He is author of Commercial Culture: The Media System and the Public Interest.

17

Courage Isn't Enough

Learning from Other People's Mistakes

John Owen

IT ALL CAME BACK TO ME in March 1984 when standing in the CBC national newsroom in Toronto: someone handed me a wire story out of El Salvador reporting that the American photographer John Hoagland had been caught in a cross fire and killed.

It was Hoagland, on assignment for *Newsweek*, who had upbraided me when I met him earlier that year outside of the Camino Real Hotel, one of those hotels forever linked in journalists' minds as the Salvador war hotel. I was then a senior journalist and field producer for a CBC TV news team that had been in San Salvador long enough to get press credentials, a translator and a van that we'd loaded with our gear. We were ready to roll out and find some "bang-bang." I introduced myself to Hoagland and asked him a few questions about where the fighting was taking place. But what I got in return were expletives: "You fucking TV guys. You come in here and think that you can just head out somewhere without first doing your homework," or something to that effect.

"Do you have any idea where you are going? You are heading right into a contested area that is dangerous!" He shook his head and abruptly walked away. I was shaken. I should have known better. I was also jolted back to reality. I realized that, in my eagerness to demonstrate my gutsiness to our correspondent who'd never been to Salvador and our TV crew, I was about to put us all at risk. It was a sobering exchange, so instead of looking for bang-bang that day, we spent our time cruising the outskirts of San Salvador.

Yet the irony wasn't lost on me when I thought about that incident and then about Hoagland's death. He knew what he was doing—he didn't take foolish chances—and still he lost his life because he'd got himself caught in a cross fire trying, like most remarkable still photographers, to get as close to the action as possible. Our Freedom Forum Journalists Memorial that honors journalists who've been killed on assignment carries this note about Hoagland: "The last two pictures in his camera show the ground swirling up to meet the falling photographer, who kept his finger on the shutter until he died."

IF EGO GOT IN THE WAY of the safety of me and my crew in El Salvador, then it was stupidity that nearly did me in at the conclusion in 1983 of the bloody Shouf war in the mountains above Beirut. Again on assignment for the CBC, breaking from my inside responsibilities as the executive producer of our flagship news program, "The National," I wanted to test myself back in the field. I volunteered to relieve the CBC's exhausted field producer who had done a long and dangerous stint in Beirut. At the time, well before the Balkans had replaced the Middle East as the most unstable region of the world, the Lebanese civil war, fought against the backdrop of an Israeli-PLO showdown with its TV pictures of the ruins of Beirut, dominated international news coverage.

But several weeks after arriving there, a cease-fire was negotiated, and the fighting among the warring factions in the Shouf Mountains, once home to popular ski resorts, was finally called to a bloody halt.

On the day that the cease-fire went into effect, the correspondent and I decided that the story could best be told, and given an important Canadian angle, by driving to the mountain village of Kfar Matta, where some of the most ferocious fighting had taken place and where the Canadian correspondent Clark Todd, who worked for a rival TV network, had been killed—perhaps murdered—earlier in the war. If peace was restored there, we thought, there was indeed some hope that it might last.

But to get to the village and back in time to edit and feed our piece by satellite that evening, we had to leave early, shoot quickly and race back. My colleagues back in Toronto had heard me rail about the sin of missing a feed deadline, and I felt under enormous self-imposed pressure to make sure that we delivered this story on time.

While driving up into the mountains we spotted what appeared to be a convoy of open trucks, filled with refugees and their belongings, headed for their home villages. It would make an excellent opening establishing shot, and our cameraman and soundman jumped out to record it.

Suddenly the convoy came to a halt. Across the road from where I had remained by our van, I could see that our cameraman and soundman were now being held by someone, not a fighter, who appeared to be waving a pistol at them. He gestured quite wildly and seemed to demand our camera. While it didn't appear that any of us was in danger, this disruption was eating into our scarce time to get to the village. While our cameraman and soundman tried to reason with the man, I noted that our camera was unattended and that I might just be able to retrieve it. But as I made my move, the man wielding the pistol moved rapidly in my direction and pointed the pistol at me. He fired, I dropped—as I understand is a natural reflex—to a fetal position. I assumed that I'd been killed or was about to be. But the man had fired off to one side.

Alive and in shock, the next thing I knew we were all surrounded by members of one of the warring Shouf factions, a jeep full of armed Druze militia. They had watched this drama unfold and swept in once they saw what was about to happen.

The man, a thieving carpet merchant who didn't want pictures of his booty or him recorded was disarmed and taken away. Hours later we got our camera back, slightly damaged and inoperative, and we were released from custody. There was now no prospect of traveling on to Kfar Matta. We returned to the famed Commodore Hotel to regroup and to see about getting our camera repaired.

I AM UNCOMFORTABLE telling these stories. They undermine the pride I felt at the time, thinking that I enjoyed a reputation of sorts for being willing to put myself at risk in these dangerous war zones, and they highlight the clumsiness and inexperience that marked my forays into hostile environments. As I reflect on these ventures, I think that what propelled me was a mixture of motives, ranging from a personal need to come to terms with never having served in Vietnam, owing to a medical deferment, to a professional sense of curiosity about what was really happening in the trouble spots of the world. Both of these impulses sent me toward zones of danger, but neither would have given me the slightest sort of survival skills once there.

Also, when I look back on what took me to a war or two as a producer for the CBC and a risky stint at the Three Mile Island nuclear power station that was presumed about to blow up, I was, even at the time of these episodes, aware that it wouldn't hurt my news career to be on these high-profile assignments. I had already figured out that those who'd been in the field enjoyed more status than those who'd never put themselves on the line covering conflicts. That was a conventional journalistic wisdom of the times, and in most major news organizations—whether it was *The New York Times*, CBS News or the CBC—you could often trace how national editors or executive producers had held foreign bureau positions or been on major international assignments before assuming managerial positions.

As I moved up the CBC executive ladder myself, I shared that viewpoint. When I became chief news editor of the CBC, I tended to appoint to senior positions those journalists who were aware of the risks and dangers that they were asking others to take in the field. I also shared a view common for those times that someone's refusal of any assignment to a potentially dangerous area smacked of cowardice, especially if that person willingly accepted pleasant assignments to exotic locales. In fact, I was determined to fire the French soundman who worked out of our Paris bureau because he had refused to accompany the cameraman to several conflicts. But the sound recordist had French law on his side, and I proved unsuccessful in sacking him.

LOOKING BACK ON THOSE two experiences in El Salvador and Lebanon—and there are other examples where I also did ill-advised things—I realize that the willingness to go into dangerous places was not enough to guarantee my safety, the safety of anyone who worked with me or our ability to capture an important story and bring it home to our viewers. We all desperately needed the kind of training for "hostile environments" that is now readily available in Britain for journalists who are about to be dispatched to their first conflict.

Until the BBC developed these courses—working closely with ex-British soldiers who realized that there was a genuine need (and good business opportunity) to sell their soldier survival skills to journalists—there was nothing in the way of training for anyone heading out the door to cover a civil war or a natural disaster. If you'd been in the military yourself, you had some sense of readiness, or if you were an avid camper, you had some idea of how to protect yourself and handle adversity. But in the words of British news photographer Gary Knight, if you were neither, "You became experienced by surviving your first assignment."

If you were lucky, you were never confronted with life-and-death decisions that tested your resourcefulness. But if you were unlucky or stupid—as I'd been in Lebanon—you called on reserves that simply weren't there.

But Andrew Kain, an ex-Special Air Service soldier who can rightly lay claim to being the founding father of these battlefield-training courses, feels that too many deaths of journalists attributed to "being at the wrong place at the wrong time" are in reality a result of misjudgments, the kind of misjudgments that I made. Too often, Kain feels, journalists tragically "took the wrong road" or didn't pick up danger signals that are part of a hyperawareness that the training courses help to engender.

Kain acknowledges that some of the highest-profile journalists take excessive risks but that those who live to report their stories make careful calculations and also may just be plain lucky, even if they've never sat through one of his courses. But Kain, an amateur military historian, quotes Otto von Bismarck: "Only a fool learns from experience. I learn from other people's mistakes."

Kain and I talked about the differences between time-honored (and prize-honored) journalistic risk taking and dangerously foolish courage at the end of a Marshall Center-organized conference in Dubrovnik, Croatia, on "military and media relations." After Kain and I parted, I returned to my room and resumed reading former foreign correspondent Peter Maass' book, *Love Thy Neighbor: A Story of War*, about the Bosnian war. (I was about to go to Bosnia for the first time, having been stuck in London as bureau chief along with other CBC duties.)

I resumed reading precisely where Maass describes his decision to drive down a dirt road that a Muslim villager told him would lead to a Serb-run prison camp. "We returned to the car and discussed the desirability of heading down the dirt track. Should we give it a shot? The answer was obviously no." Maass then says, "And so we headed down the dirt road."

Maass and his companions were soon spotted, and he was convinced they would be executed in the remote surrounding cornfields. But miraculously, they were released. Maass in telling the story says: "I was also dismayed by the realization that I had the capacity to act like a crazy SOB, despite my better judgment. The degree of stupidity in heading down that dirt track cannot be measured."

But Maass said that he, like so many other driven journalists, was like a "bloodhound on the scent of a fox" and was determined to get to the camps to see for himself what was being done to Bosnian Muslims. He did later accomplish that mission and gave the world the benefit of his eyewitness reports.

DURING THE KOSOVO CONFLICT, all Western journalists, save one—Canadian Paul Watson reporting for the *Los Angeles Times*—did the sensible and safe thing and stayed out of Kosovo once NATO started its bombing campaign. But Watson felt that in good conscience he couldn't remain outside and went right back in and continued to file throughout the war. Said Watson (who was awarded the George Polk Award in 1999 for his reporting of the war in Kosovo) in a piece reflecting on what he'd done: "The few colleagues who knew what I was doing said I was insane. My wife understood that I had to go back. So I went. It would probably take a psychiatrist to really understand why I felt compelled to return and offer Serbs an easy target for revenge against Westerners but everyone has his own ghosts." And Watson is one of the few correspondents who says openly that some stories are worth dying for. In a March 2000 Freedom Forum debate in London on the coverage of Kosovo he said that "I don't wish death on anybody, but in this business if you choose to do it, the first decision you have to make is: "'I'm willing to make the sacrifice.'"

I did put the question to a Canadian psychiatrist, one who himself has been under fire and is fascinated by what motivates journalists to take the risks they do. Dr. Anthony Feinstein, a South African by birth, served as a medical officer during the bloody Namibian conflict in 1984. He kept a diary, later published in a small book called In Conflict. Feinstein, who distinguished himself in his medical work in the conflict, is greatly admiring of those journalists who do feel a higher calling and are willing to put their lives on the line: "I would put it to you that journalists who go to extraordinary lengths to report the truth obviously show a greater degree of personal courage and are motivated by a strong sense of personal justice." Dr. Feinstein, who practices psychiatry at the University of Toronto's Sunnybrook Hospital, does worry, however, about the long-term consequences for many journalists who have witnessed too much horror and destruction. He and The Freedom Forum are about to embark on the most ambitious study yet done of journalists who may be suffering from what is referred to as post-traumatic stress syndrome.

For Andrew Kain, the ex-soldier, and for me, the former CBC producer, some of the most impressively brave journalism is practiced by local journalists who somehow find the inner strength to continue publishing newspapers and broadcasting reports that daily put them in harm's way. When I met up with Kain in Dubrovnik, he had just arrived from Podgorica, Montenegro, where he'd staged a version of the safety course, underwritten by The Freedom Forum, for 10 independent journalists from Serbia—many of them from the embattled B-92 news group of Belgrade (now called B-292) and five from Montenegro. They are at the knife edge of the Balkans conflict and face daily unrelenting pressure, physical intimidation and death threats. Kain is in awe of their willingness to keep going, especially given how little they're paid—well under $100 a month in most places. On Kain's "courage meter" this kind of risk taking ranks higher than any other journalism that he's encountered. But can it be foolish as well?

When Kain and I were having our conversation in Dubrovnik, a young Bulgarian correspondent, Boyko Vassilev, from Bulgarian National Television joined us. He has covered, along with a cameraman, the conflicts in the Balkans by driving from Sofia, Bulgaria, staying in hostels and transporting his own canisters of gasoline. He speaks seven languages so he doesn't need to hire translators.

Asked whether what he was doing was courageous or foolish, Vassilev whose first name means war in Bulgarian, said that "true courage is never foolish."

"It's a calculation you make," he said. "And when it's 50-50 or worse, then you don't go."

John Owen was chief news editor of CBC Television News and chief of foreign bureaus based in London before joining The Freedom Forum as European director.

18

Freedom Neruda

Struggles for Press Freedom in West Africa

W. Joseph Campbell

THE OFFENDING ARTICLE was tucked away on page 10 of *La Voie*, an opposition daily newspaper in Côte d'Ivoire in West Africa. The piece carried a provocative headline: "Il maudit l'ASEC"—"He jinxed ASEC." The article's contents were more provocative—and criminally insulting under Ivorian law.

It declared that by attending the All-Africa championship soccer match in Abidjan, the commercial capital of Côte d'Ivoire, then Ivorian president, Henri Konan Bédié, had brought bad luck to the host (and losing) team, the ASEC Mimosas. The article recalled and poked fun at Bédié's campaign literature from the year before. Bédié had boasted that his presidency had brought good fortune to Côte d'Ivoire, a former French colony that styled itself an island of political stability in an otherwise troubled corner of the world.

The article about Bédié's jinxing the country's soccer team would lead to a jail term and ultimately to a measure of international fame for its author, Roch d'Assomption Tiéti, who writes under the nom de plume Freedom Neruda. He chose the name because he found inspiring the work of the Chilean poet Pablo Neruda.

The case of Freedom Neruda is in several respects emblematic of the quiet courage of journalists in French-speaking West Africa, a region where a surprisingly resilient—yet little recognized—ethos of independent journalism has emerged and taken hold since the early 1990s. Hundreds of newspapers published independently of government control have appeared across the region. More recently, scores of privately owned radio stations have taken to the airwaves.

To be sure, casualty rates for the emergent news media have been substantial. Most of the newspapers have failed, usually falling victim to a combination of official crackdowns, revenue shortfalls, material shortages, and inadequate professional training and development programs. But many titles have defied the odds to establish themselves as features of a robust and increasingly pluralist media landscape.

The astonishing change in the region's media scene was set in motion by a broad-based wave of democratization that embraced much of sub-Saharan Africa in the late 1980s and early 1990s, coinciding with but largely unrelated to the political upheaval that swept Eastern and Central Europe and the former Soviet Union. While the emergence of news media independent of government control was dependent upon the wider process of political liberalization, the development and vitality of those media are attributable primarily to journalists, such as Freedom Neruda, who, for reasons including the limited circulation of their publications, are little known outside the region. Their searching, sometimes-partisan, independent-minded journalism has had the effect of expanding open consideration of issues and policies in countries where debate and dissenting views had been severely restricted or even forbidden by single-party regimes. In some cases, newspapers have been contributing factors in the repudiation of national leaders whose democratic credentials proved thin, dubious or illusory.

The development of independent-minded journalism has not been without its flaws and shortcomings, however. Newspapers independent of government control have been known to be swaggering in their assertiveness and shrill in their partisanship. The founders of *La Voie* described themselves as "animated by a will comparable to that of the Vietnamese in their war against the Americans." Though hyperbolic, the reference is a revealing example of the earnestness that has been associated with the emergent independent press in West Africa. More troubling has been corruption of journalists, usually in the form of payoffs from news sources. Accepting payoffs in exchange for flattering or favorable articles has proved an enduring and recurring problem in many countries, one driven by a combination of meager salaries, an uncertain sense of ethical boundaries and limited professional training programs. To confront such practices, journalists in Côte d'Ivoire and in Benin have established self-regulating monitoring or watchdog panels called observatoires, which meet periodically to call attention to lapses in professional conduct. The effectiveness of such panels is open to challenge, but the Ivorian observatoire appears to have achieved a broad measure of support among journalists since its founding in the mid-1990s.

BUT BY FAR the most severe threat to the region's independent-minded journalists is the never-distant prospect that their reporting will lead to harassment, intimidation and even imprisonment. Nearly all West African states have conducted multiparty elections since 1990, but only Benin and Mali were, at the end of the decade, home to a free press, according to quantitative rankings compiled by New York-based Freedom House. Journalists have been jailed or newspapers have been suspended in nearly every country where an independent press has emerged in French-speaking West Africa—Benin, Burkina Faso, Cameroon, Chad, Côte d'Ivoire, Guinea, Mali, Niger and Togo. In the five years after *La Voie*'s founding in 1991, no fewer than a half dozen of the newspaper's editorial staff were sentenced to prison for their reporting.

The article that led to the jailing of Freedom Neruda appeared in *La Voie* in December 1995. A companion piece, written by Emmanuel Koré, suggested the president should have stayed home the night of the soccer championship match. While the articles were scarcely the most inflammatory to have appeared in *La Voie* (the name of which was changed in 1998 to *Notre Voie*, or Our Way), they did pose direct challenges to the stature and even the authority of Bédié, the head of state. As such, they represented challenges to the state itself.

Freedom Neruda, Koré and the newspaper's publication director, Abou Drahamane Sangaré, were arrested, quickly brought to trial on charges of insulting the head of state, pronounced guilty and sentenced to two years in prison. For offenses so trivial, the penalties were exceptional, and their severity stirred an international outcry. Amnesty International, for example, said it appeared that the Ivorian legal system was "being used . . . to stifle the opposition press and restrict its right to freedom of expression."

Ivorian officials sought to justify jailing Freedom Neruda and his colleagues by insisting that the head of state is the embodiment of national unity and dignity and must be insulated from unflattering and objectionable commentary. What's more, said then-minister of communications, Danièle Boni-Claverie: "Our press is sick. We have to cure it of the sickness so that it does not contaminate the others."

Freedom Neruda, Koré, and Sangaré were ordered to serve their sentences at the MACA, the French-language acronym for the forbidding house of corrections in Abidjan. Cholera and other diseases are known to run rampant at times at the MACA, a grim place built to house 1,500 prisoners. By the mid-1990s, the inmate population had swollen to more than 5,400.

Freedom Neruda, Koré and Sangaré served half of their two-year sentences and were quietly released at the New Year 1997. Much as other journalists who have been jailed in the region, they emerged saying they had not been cowed by the ordeal of imprisonment, that their views had only grown stronger. Within 10 months of his release, Freedom Neruda was on his way to the United States and a black-tie dinner at the Waldorf-Astoria Hotel in New York, where he accepted an International Press Freedom Award from the Committee to Protect Journalists. Freedom Neruda was one of six journalists so honored in 1997, and he noted later that whenever during his stay in the United States he recounted the circumstances that led to imprisonment—how he was jailed for insulting the president—his "audience was simply dumbfounded" that satiric commentary could be deemed a crime. (In part because of the circumstances of his jailing, Freedom Neruda was named in 2000 one of the 50 "World Press Freedom Heroes" by the International Press Institute.)

WHILE EXTRAORDINARY IN ITS DETAILS, Freedom Neruda's case reflected the hazards that confront many independent-minded journalists in French-speaking West Africa. Not infrequently do the region's journalists gain a measure of regional recognition for standing up to repression, for serving time in jail or for going to court to answer allegations of defamatory reporting. Freedom Neruda's counterparts in quiet courage are many in French-speaking West Africa and include Diégou Bailly, the publication director of Le Jour, which is perhaps the most sophisticated independent daily newspaper in Côte d'Ivoire; Maurice Chabi, the publication director of Les Echos du Jour, a leading daily in Benin, a Pennsylvania-sized country that has established itself the region's leader in democratic governance; Pius N. Njawé, the often-prosecuted publication director of *Le Messager*, which has been called "the most confrontational" newspaper in Cameroon; and Mamadou Oumar Ndiaye, publisher of an aggressive weekly newspaper in Senegal, *Le Témoin*.

The laws under which Freedom Neruda and others have been prosecuted—measures that criminalize insults and other criticism of heads of state—do not vary markedly across the region. And they have their roots in French colonial rule, which tolerated little criticism of authorities. In many cases, postcolonial West African states have modified only slightly the restrictive French model. With the notable exception of what is now Benin, independent-minded journalism was rarely seen until the closing years of French rule in West Africa.

It is thus mildly ironic that France also is the most obvious and most direct model for the independent press in francophone West Africa. The region's newspapers in some cases are styled after those in Paris. Bailly's *Le Jour* resembles the left-of-center Parisian daily *Libération* in tone and typography. And Bailly is one of many West African journalists who have studied in France. (Freedom Neruda, who was born in 1956, received a degree in sciences at the University of Abidjan in 1983 and taught mathematics for a while before entering journalism in 1988 as a trainee copy editor.)

The limited historical legacy in French-speaking West Africa of expressing dissent through the press makes the emergence of an ethos of independent journalism all the more striking. Although the trajectory of press development in the region has not been without reverses and embarrassments, the broad trends are encouraging: the independent press in many countries has moved in recent years from weekly and monthly publication to daily periodicity. Numerous independent newspapers appear daily in Benin and Côte d'Ivoire, for example—before 1990, there were no such newspapers in either country.

ANOTHER TREND HAS been the deepening recognition of the value of independent journalism in promoting respect for democratic practices. The independent press in Benin undoubtedly contributed to the popular rejection of Nicéphore Soglo, who had been chosen president in one of West Africa's first, and fairest, elections of the 1990s. Soglo, however, soon demonstrated his impatience with the untidiness and the rough-and-tumble of multiparty politics. Within a year of his election in 1991, newspapers were openly questioning whether Soglo possessed the temperament and administrative acumen required to manage Benin's fractious political culture.

Soglo proved extraordinarily sensitive to criticism, depicting himself as the target of printed attacks that were unmatched in vehemence anywhere in the world. He challenged the scruples of the country's independent press and took to upbraiding Beninese journalists, usually in telephone calls in which he remonstrated about the coverage he received. The president's telephone calls became so frequent that one journalist remarked, "We could write a book called Soglo Online."

He also invited criticism in his high-handed relations with the National Assembly. He announced cabinet changes without first consulting with the speaker of the parliament, as the Beninese constitution required. Former supporters in the legislature accused him of treating the National Assembly as a rubber stamp and indulging in a "solitary exercise" in wielding power.

By the time Soglo stood for re-election in 1996, his credentials as a reform-minded democrat were widely questioned—a development that was attributable in measure to the sustained scrutiny of the independent press. The newspapers had withstood pressure from Soglo and his supporters to soften or alter their reporting and, by revealing the president as a dubious democrat, helped prepare for his rejection at the polls.

Soglo finished first in the opening round of voting in March 1996 but failed to gain a majority. Soglo's opponents rallied around Benin's former military ruler, a born-again Christian named Mathieu Kérékou—the man whom Soglo defeated in the 1991 elections. This time, Kérékou won the runoff.

Soglo raged at the outcome, appealing to the Constitutional Court to overturn the result. He described himself as the victim of "a vast conspiracy" and of a "national and international media lynching" to deny him a second term. In the end, Soglo's appeal was rejected. Benin peacefully changed chief executives for the second time in many presidential elections—outcomes unprecedented in postcolonial West Africa.

THAT INDEPENDENT JOURNALISTS CAN, through persistent and critical reporting, present compelling evidence of flawed or failed political leadership was demonstrated anew in Côte d'Ivoire in the late 1990s. By then, Henri Konan Bédié, the Ivorian president and Freedom Neruda's jailer, had become more autocratic. Democratic rule in Côte d'Ivoire seemed more chimerical than ever. Bédié had won passage of a constitutional amendment, prolonging presidential terms to seven from five years. But as the campaigning began for presidential elections scheduled in 2000, a formidable rival to Bédié loomed. He was Alassane D. Ouattara, formerly an Ivorian prime minister and senior official at the International Monetary Fund.

Bédié turned to a variety of repressive measures to block Ouattara's candidacy, claiming notably that he failed to meet nationality requirements to stand for the Ivorian presidency. When Ouattara produced documents showing that he and his parents were of Ivorian nationals, Bédié's government ordered his arrest on the grounds the documents were forged. Meanwhile, 11 leaders of Ouattara's party had been sent to prison following a demonstration against what they said was biased reporting at the state-run broadcast outlets.

Notre Voie, Le Jour and the country's other nonofficial newspapers reported closely on the deepening political drama, thus contributing to a widening recognition of Bédié's intolerance. The president's repudiation finally came not at the polls but in the country's first-ever coup d'état. The Ivorian military seized power on Christmas Eve 1999, promising a return to democratic rule through free and fair elections. Although such promises are commonplace in the aftermath of military takeovers, politicking in Côte d'Ivoire almost immediately resumed in earnest.

Bédié, meanwhile, took refuge at the French embassy in Abidjan and later was allowed to leave the country with a small entourage. He visited Togo and Nigeria in a halfhearted, ultimately futile attempt to rally support from other West Africa states. He retreated to Paris, suggesting he might present himself in the elections that the military promised but had not yet scheduled as of March 2000.

Perhaps as a measure of respect for the Ivorian press, the military authorities made no move to silence or repress the independent newspapers, which overwhelmingly welcomed Bédié's ouster. *Notre Voie*, for example, hailed the coup as a case of the "gods [having] offered the Côte d'Ivoire a chance to make a new start, an opportunity few countries are accorded." (The military rulers demonstrated little tolerance for another setback in Ivorian soccer, however. After the national team was eliminated in the first round of the 2000 African Cup of

Nations tournament, the players were taken to a military camp for three days of workouts.)

For Freedom Neruda, the Christmas Eve coup meant that he had outlasted his nemesis and jailer. About a month afterward, he was promoted to assistant editor in chief, the second-ranking editorial post at *Notre Voie*.

But he resisted gloating about Bédié's demise. Rather than celebrating the fall of the man who had sent him to the MACA, Freedom Neruda wrote about the importance of reconciliation. He expressed his "profound sense of pity" for senior officials of Bédié's government who were arrested and briefly detained after the coup. Freedom Neruda described them as "mortal and vulnerable men who some people had believed to be demi-gods."

In any case, score-settling was unnecessary, Freedom Neruda wrote. "The people have no need to avenge themselves. To the contrary, they should stand above that and offer a pardon to those [officials] who failed to understand that no star shines forever."

Besides, he wrote, "What good does it do to take shots at the ambulance of a sick man who is in an irreversible coma? Let's learn to show some pity."

W. Joseph Campbell, a former wire service reporter in West Africa, teaches journalism at American University. He is author of The Emergent Independent Press in Benin and Côte d'Ivoire: From Voice of the State to Advocate of Democracy.

Review Essay

Different Faces of Courage

19

Who Has Guts?

Tough Questions about Morality and Bravery

James Boylan

EACH YEAR, THE NEW YORK-BASED Committee to Protect Journalists convenes to honor journalists from around the world who have demonstrated extraordinary courage and independence. (Of the four 1999 recipients, one was in prison and another in exile.) CPJ offers an additional award, in memory of Burton Benjamin, an esteemed CBS News producer and a chairman of CPJ; it usually honors the already much-honored.

In 1997, the recipient of the Benjamin award was Ted Koppel of ABC News, who refreshingly chose to examine the varieties of courage that journalism might demand and that its practitioners might or might not supply. He paid tribute to the award winners from abroad: "They function, when they can, at the risk of their freedom and often their lives." He counted himself among those called on to display a second type of courage—the correspondents who "have worked in dangerous places and have certainly taken risks." He added: "The risks we took tended to be overseas. We could always come home."

But for America's at-home journalism he had words of scorn, charging that it lacked a particular kind of courage—the strength to challenge its audience:

It is not death, or torture or imprisonment that threatens us as American journalists, it is the trivialization of our industry. We are free to write

169

and report whatever we believe is important. But if what is important does not appeal to the reading or viewing appetites of our consumers we'll give them something that does. . . . we're afraid of the competition; afraid of earning less money; afraid of losing our audience. They face death and torture and imprisonment; and we are afraid.

Everything Koppel said about trivialization, about the fear of competition was borne out, in spades, during the subsequent Year of Lewinsky. And yet, looking closely at his admonishment, one wonders just who is the "we" he refers to as American journalists. Koppel's "we" is clearly managerial by implication; the practices he deplores rest on profit-driven, audience-driven corporate policies—not usually the province of the working reporter or editor. Another type of courage is conspicuous by its omission: that is, the willingness of individuals to define and defend their own standards while operating in an organizational setting. This kind of courage was evoked in the statement issued earlier in 1997 by the Committee of Concerned Journalists, which said, essentially, that employees could no longer depend on owners and managers to articulate journalists' responsibilities, and that practitioners must speak out to define their own purposes and principles.

Thus, we find three or four types of courage: the courage to resist legal and physical threats on one's native ground, the courage to risk danger to tell disquieting news to the world of the comfortable, the corporate courage to offer audiences what they do not necessarily want to hear, and the courage to become a dissident inside an organization.

CPJ's MAIN BUSINESS, calling attention to persecution of journalists around the world, is delineated in its annual report, *Attacks on the Press* in 1999. It offers abundant examples of physical courage— journalists facing intimidation, kidnapping, physical assaults, imprisonment, torture, death. But the report does not go everywhere; it has nothing at all to say on the apparently unafflicted media of Western Europe, Britain, Japan and Canada. Nor does it offer much on the United States, except to note attacks on the immigrant press and death threats issued to the free-lancer Robert Friedman by Russian gangsters—essentially phenomena imported from the other world.

That other world, CPJ makes clear, remains perilous ground for independent journalism. Governments combine the ancient legal weapons of licensing and criminal libel with secret-police methods. Outlaw factions—criminal, religious, political—carry on wars of their own. CPJ reports 34 assassinations last year—that is, individuals killed because they were journalists: 10 in a burst of revolutionary violence in tiny Sierra Leone, six in Yugoslavia, five in Colombia. Just an average year, perhaps slightly sub-average; since 1990, 458 have been killed in 56 countries. Moreover, as of the end of 1999, 87 remained in prison, and many others have been forced into exile. These are only the most visible cases, far outnumbered by hundreds threatened by actions designed to obstruct and terrorize.

There is a seeming gulf between the protected world of the technologically advanced journalism of what could be called the North Atlantic civilization and the generally smaller-scale journalism of the rest of the world. In many countries, journalism is still struggling to gain independence and find its place in societies that are not accustomed to independent scrutiny, may not welcome it and may try to destroy those who attempt it.

American journalists, wrapped in a usually protective legal and cultural tradition, may regard the struggles in Africa, Asia, Latin America and Eastern Europe as peculiarly alien. But there was a time when America was not that different. In his innovative 1994 study, *Violence Against the Press*, John Nerone paints a historical landscape that will be unfamiliar to those brought up on conventional onward-and-upward texts about newspaper history. Nerone destroys the notion that attacks on the press and on journalists in America are anomalous, mere "episodes and accidents." Rather, he finds that they have been endemic, "an integral part of the culture of public expression in the United States." Mob action, he asserts, was a means of channeling, even regulating the press. His evidence is plentiful—for example, continual assaults on the abolitionist press, 111 instances of mob actions against newspapers during the Civil War and cases stretching into this century of attacks on the minority, ethnic, labor and left press.

Reading Nerone and the CPJ report in juxtaposition, one can readily imagine that today's throng of journalists around the world, struggling to maintain their right to speak or to print, are spiritual successors to the American printers and editors of preceding centuries—the wartime dissidents, abolitionists, radicals and unionists who asserted, in the abolitionist publisher William Lloyd Garrison's words, "I will be heard!" And to tell the truth, not all the news in the CPJ report is bad; more than a few nations are slowly moving toward internationally recognized guarantees of freedom of expression. There are places where seditious-libel laws have been replaced by legislation assuring the right to criticize governments and officials with impunity. Just as in the United States, American printers and editors staked the early claims for freedom of the press by simply continuing to publish and assert their rights, those on other continents are now winning for themselves the space to practice independent journalism.

Their courage is self-evident. What astonishes is the breadth and persistence of their efforts. If prudence ruled, half of the world would have to do without journalists. But just the opposite is the case; countries that once had no journalism worthy of the name have spawned newspapers, magazines, television and radio stations, and, above all, men and women audacious enough to practice the craft. A few flee; most remain and risk the consequences. Clearly, they are driven by more than money or glory; instead, they see themselves as improving, cleansing their societies.

BETWEEN THE TWO WORLDS of journalism, the journalism of safe places and the journalism of dangerous places, there is a small clan that belongs truly to neither. Correspondents are employed by the West's big media engines, but they constantly expose themselves to the dangers of the other more hostile world. The 1999 CPJ report notes fatalities among these outsiders—for example, an Associated Press correspondent in Sierra Leone and a German reporter and photographer in Kosovo.

Two such intermediaries, of the type who almost compulsively seek out disorder, violence and personal danger, have recently written accounts of their work, strikingly different in character.

Leslie Cockburn has been practicing her dangerous trade for almost 25 years. She broke in at NBC in 1976 and has been employed by CBS, ABC, PBS and *Vanity Fair*. Her book speaks little about her employers; instead, she has written the classic foreign correspondent's memoir—"how I got that story." It is a breathtaking, and sometimes breathless, narrative. As the cover blurb asserts, she "has dined with the Cali Cartel, marched with the Khmer Rouge, hunted down the Black Turban in Afghanistan, pursued the Russian mafia to the Arctic

Circle, shared pomegranate sauce with the ayatollahs, and stopped a small Kurdish war."

Her narrative is informed by a political sensibility—a determination to bring to the attention of the public what it may least want to hear about the rest of the world. Her tone is optimistic, even joyous, darkened only when somebody places obstacles in the way of her mission. For example, she spent weeks preparing a story for ABC on turbulence and famine in Somalia, only to have to yield time to Koppel, flown in for the landing of American troops. Her dessicated segment "was packaged between teases, bumpers, ads for Tylenol, Ben-Gay, and a jeep parked on the edge of the Grand Canyon."

Looking for Trouble is written in the first person, but it is neither truly personal nor revelatory. Cockburn recounts even her riskiest excursions with immense cool. Although any one of a dozen ventures could have turned out badly, she says little about the risks. Her jacket blurbs suggest courage, but she takes no note of it. It is a kind of classic tough-guy approach.

By contrast, Anthony Loyd confronts the question of courage repeatedly and directly. *My War Gone By* is as painful and self-scourging as skin turned inside out. A member of a military family and briefly a soldier himself, he went to Yugoslavia in 1993 to find war, having been disappointed by what he saw in the Gulf in 1991. He had no trouble catching up with combat in Bosnia, first as a haphazardly trained, semiaccredited free-lance photographer, eventually as a military correspondent for *The Times* of London. He also made a horrendous side trip to the first war in Chechnya.

That he managed to become a journalist while fighting off personal crises—his father's hostility and death, a serious drug addiction, psychotherapy—seems a small miracle. But at the same time personal crisis opened him to absorbing not only the facts of the war but its ethos, its ferocity, danger and unpredictability. One vignette among many: three Muslim prisoners pushed out into no-man's-land, mines strapped to their bodies and trailing wires, blown up as they approached their comrades, their legs left to lie on the field for days afterward.

Loyd conducts a continual inquest on himself. He asserts initially that going to the war had nothing to do with personal courage but was "more an absolution of self-responsibility, a releasing of myself into the hands of chance." Later, facing not merely danger but the probability of death under fire, he found that he was not willing to give away his life to happenstance. He was overcome with dread, shaken into immobility. When he had restabilized, he reflected: "I did not learn to accept courage in a different form, I grew to see it as a meaningless term of glorification used by the ignorant to describe the actions of others whose real motivations are more often instinctive than altruistic."

Clearly, he does not distinguish between the courage of a soldier and that of a journalist who happens to be on the same battlefield with soldiers. The purely journalistic courage—although he, like Leslie Cockburn, would no doubt shun the term—emerges in other terms, in his newfound passion to tell the world of the war's rights and wrongs: " . . . the writing suddenly gave me a sense of purpose. I had found the war to be as unjust as it was brutal. . . . I believed that something fundamental was at stake in the war." What fuels him in the end is not playing pseudosoldier, although he still acts the part, but exposing himself so as to expose the war.

At the same time, the war ruins him for the routines of civil life, and he is irresistibly drawn to the battlefield: "Sometimes I pray for another war just to save me." It was not surprising to read that in October 1999 Loyd was detained at the Chechnya border, no doubt still trying to mend himself by getting close enough to the fighting to hear the bullets go by.

A SURVEY THAT JOHN NERONE did for Violence Against the Press found that today's mainstream American journalism inspires only scattered incidents of violence or threatened violence. Most journalists in America no longer consider their work physically dangerous, despite having to deal with a quotient of anger from those who believe their privacy or right to be heard has been violated. Nerone suggests that in general journalism no longer stimulates an aggressive public response. What was once a public has been reduced to an audience. Publics act; audiences consume.

What they consume is the well-packaged work of those who consider themselves professionals. Nerone believes that professionalism itself has insulated journalism from the public. Journalists once were participants in the public life of local communities; now they operate—particularly those in the national news media—by a "set of codes and cues that only insiders can master" barricaded within their organizations.

This notion of the journalist as insider places a paradoxical twist on the title of the Michael Mann film, *The Insider*, released late in 1999. The film deals with the difficulties a "60 Minutes" producer encountered in seeking to put a major tobacco whistle-blower on the air. Clearly, the insider of the title is Jeffrey Wigand, the scientist from Brown & Williamson who decided to go public. At the same time, though, Lowell Bergman, the "60 Minutes" producer who found and worked with Wigand, is also an insider, encountering dilemmas of personal and professional integrity within CBS strikingly parallel to those faced by Wigand. In the end, the Bergman character, too, becomes a whistle-blower.

The Insider is said to be based primarily on an article by Marie Brenner, "The Man Who Knew Too Much," which appeared in the May 1996 issue of *Vanity Fair*. She tells how Wigand was fired by Brown & Williamson for, essentially, unwillingness to go along with the fiction that tobacco companies did not know that their products were addictive. Wigand knew in fact that Brown & Williamson sought additives to enhance cigarettes' addictiveness. He became known to "60 Minutes" more or less by chance and, after months of courtship, agreed in the summer of 1995 to be interviewed on camera. He had to abandon his confidentiality agreements with his former employer; not incidentally, his marriage dissolved under pressures of financial insecurity and, apparently, threats against his children.

In October 1995, CBS legal counsel directed "60 Minutes" not to broadcast the interview—and to break off all contact with Wigand—on the ground that CBS could be sued by Brown & Williamson for "tortious interference" with Wigand's confidentiality agreements. In the background was the pending sale of CBS to Westinghouse, a conglomerate with tobacco connections; the film makes a point of listing out the millions that would be harvested by those involved in killing the Wigand interview. Not mentioned, but probably of much more importance, is the expensive settlement that Capital Cities/ABC had just made with another tobacco giant, Philip Morris, and its retraction of a broadcast charging that Philip Morris had hyped nicotine levels. Not until the *Wall Street Journal* obtained and published Wigand's secret data (without mentioning Wigand by name) and CBS had been publicly embarrassed by exposure of its self-censorship did Wigand's interview appear in its original form. The *Journal* won a Pulitzer for its efforts; CBS reaped embarrassment.

As a film, this tale is not a paean to journalism like *All the President's Men*. Yet here it is, 158 minutes of it, and in its way, I suppose, as true to real life in the 1990s as the Woodstein saga was to newspapering in the 1970s. *The Insider* offers little guts and glory; it is all moral quandaries—not only Wigand's, but those faced or avoided by television newspeople.

UNAVOIDABLY, MUCH OF THE DISCUSSION of this film, which purports to represent real events, has centered on its factual fidelity. Certain participants, notably Mike Wallace, claim to have been misrepresented. A workaday "60 Minutes" producer, Lowell Bergman, is glamorized and enlarged by the superstar Al Pacino. And the techniques are indubitably those of fiction film—dancing cameras, spectacular settings, wrenching music and innumerable shifts of chronology and detail. But as best as this outsider can determine, by comparing the film with both the Brenner article and, especially, the exhaustive narrative of the crisis at CBS in Lawrence K. Grossman's January/February 1996 *Columbia Journalism Review* article, "CBS, '60 Minutes,' and the Unseen Interview," many essentials are there in the film: that Bergman made a solemn commitment to put Wigand on the air, that CBS killed the Wigand interview under an apparently unprecedented, perhaps imagined, threat of a lawsuit; and that, ultimately, CBS tried to leave Wigand twisting in the wind.

The film invidiously nominates heroes and nonheroes at CBS. Bergman, in true Pacino style, is unwavering. His colleagues are weaker, depending on their distance from the top. Wallace is shown as willing to go along with management's decision, but eventually turns around. Don Hewitt, the executive producer, is shown as a patsy (a portrait that Bergman hinted, in an interview, was unfair). The head of CBS News, given a fictional name, is portrayed as a spineless supporter of management. The chief CBS lawyer, also given a fictional identity, is a straight-out heavy. But to a viewer of the film these nuances of compliance do not matter a lot. Who would expect that a corporation, in a matter involving millions or perhaps billions, to have at its heart a conscience, rather than prudence? And who would expect its deputies, even those engaged in journalism, to dissent or disobey?

Indeed, that is the question, and the dilemma faced by the film's Bergman. How far before disagreement becomes dissent? And before loyal dissent becomes disloyal? And to whom and to what is loyalty owed? The Bergman played by Pacino is not a particularly reflective person; he simply keeps fighting to get his story out and to keep faith with Wigand.

Ultimately, what is portrayed as his climactic act of rebellion is leaking the story of CBS's self-censorship to a *New York Times* reporter, played by Pete Hamill of all people. Curiously, most real-life accounts of the affair slide by the leak as incidental and do not even attribute it to Bergman. Yet it did occur, and it resulted in a Page One *Times* story on November 9, 1995, by television-beat reporter Bill Carter.

The leak was glancingly acknowledged by Bergman himself in an interview with David Weir in the on-line magazine *Salon* on November 5, 1999: " . . . in the movie, it's clear I leaked the story to The New York Times that made it all public. You know, so that is true."

Was this an act of courage or a dirty, even traitorous tactic? In the film, Christopher Plummer as Wallace rebukes Pacino/Bergman, more in sorrow than in anger, for an act of disloyalty. If it is, it is hardly unprecedented. Warren Breed's still illuminating old study, "Social Control in the Newsroom," found that reporters caught in tight policy situations often subverted management, customarily by leaking to another organization on the unspoken premise that the public was entitled to know.

The question is always the urgency of the need to know. Although Bergman (in the film) clearly had personal reasons to try to break out the story—his belief that he had failed Wigand and his chagrin over losing exclusivity—the substantive side of the story was also of extraordinary importance in shaking the tobacco industry from its long-term position of denial on smoking and health. But eventually the story of the network's self-censorship loomed almost as large as the tobacco angle.

Bergman's actions are (were?) ambivalent. The film—which Bergman called in the *Salon* interview his "final act as a whistle-blower"—emphasizes his courage in going outside the rules of the game. Yet he can be viewed as reckless (he could have been fired) or self-aggrandizing (he could have become what Plummer/Wallace calls a "First Amendment martyr.")

But perhaps every act of journalistic courage contains such a duality. Loyd offers himself with infinite nerve on battlefields, but at the same time he gets the fix he wants most—war.

The apparently purest form of journalistic courage, displayed by those that CPJ seeks to defend on other continents, may be mixed with politics, personal ambition and even personality defects. Even the sainted William Lloyd Garrison was regarded by his contemporaries as Boston's leading crank. We probably will never find courage unalloyed, and we need to accept it for what it offers.

James Boylan, professor emeritus of journalism at the University of Massachusetts-Amherst, was founding editor of the Columbia Journalism Review.

For Further Reading

Albert, Pierre. La France, les États-Unis et leurs Presses: 1632-1976. Paris: Centre Georges Pompidou, 1977.

Allen, James, ed. Without Sanctuary: Lynching Photography in America. Santa Fe, N.M.: Twin Palms, 1999.

Balk, Alfred, and James Boylan, eds. Our Troubled Press: Ten Years of the Columbia Journalism Review. Boston: Little, Brown, 1971.

Bogart, Leo. Commercial Culture: The Media System and the Public Interest. New Brunswick, N.J.: Transaction Publishers, 2000.

Camus, Albert. Between Hell and Reason: Essays from the Resistance Newspaper Combat, 1944-1947. Translated by Alexandre de Gramont. Hanover, N.H.: Wesleyan University Press/ University Press of New England, 1991.

Capa, Robert. Slightly out of Focus. New York: Modern Library, 1999.

Cockburn, Leslie. Looking for Trouble: One Woman, Six Wars, and a Revolution. New York: Anchor Books/Doubleday, 1999.

Committee to Protect Journalists. Attacks on the Press in 1999. New York: CPJ, 2000.

Copeland, David A. Debating the Issues in Colonial Newspapers: Primary Documents on Events of the Period. Westport, Conn.: Greenwood Press, 2000.

———. Colonial American Newspapers: Character and Content. Newark, Del.: University of Delaware Press, 1997.

Coward, John M. The Newspaper Indian: Native American Identity in the Press, 1820-90. Urbana, Ill.: University of Illinois Press, 1999.

Currie, Stephen. The Liberator: Voice of the Abolitionist Movement. San Diego, Calif: Lucent Books, 2000.

Duzán, María Jimena. Death Beat: A Colombian Journalist's Life Inside the Cocaine Wars. Translated by Peter Eisner. New York: Harper Collins, 1994.

García Márquez, Gabriel. News of a Kidnapping. Translated by Edith Grossman. New York: Knopf, 1997.

Goldstein, Tom, ed. Killing the Messenger: 100 Years of Media Criticism. New York: Columbia University Press, 1989.

Gutiérrez, Félix. Race, Multiculturalism, and the Media: From Mass to Class Communication. Thousand Oaks, Calif.: Sage Publications, 1995.

Hodges, Graham Russell. Root and Branch: African Americans in New York and East Jersey, 1613-1863. Chapel Hill, N.C.: University of North Carolina Press, 1999.

Holland, Jack. Hope Against History: The Course of Conflict in Northern Ireland. New York: Henry Holt, 1999.

Hong, Nathaniel. Sparks of Resistance: The Illegal Press in German-Occupied Denmark, April 1940-August 1943. Odense, Denmark: Odense University Press, 1996.

Hurley, Frank. Shackleton's Argonauts, A Saga of the Antarctic Ice-Packs. Sydney, Australia: Angus and Robertson, 1948.

Katz, Stanley Nider, and James Alexander, eds. A Brief Narrative of the Case and Trial of John Peter Zenger, Printer of The New York Weekly Journal. Cambridge, Mass.: Belknap Press of Harvard University Press, 1963.

Kepner, Jim. Rough News, Daring Views: 1950s' Pioneer Gay Press Journalism. New York: Harrington Park Press, 1998.

Kneebone, John T. Southern Liberal Journalists and the Issue of Race, 1920-1944. Chapel Hill, N.C.: University of North Carolina Press, 1985.

Lacy, Sam, and Moses J. Newson. Fighting for Fairness: The Life Story of Hall of Fame Sportswriter Sam Lacy. Centreville, Md.: Tidewater Publishers, 1998.

Lieven, Anatol. Chechnya: Tombstone of Russian Power. New Haven, Conn.: Yale University Press, 1998.

Loyd, Anthony. My War Gone By, I Miss It So. New York: Atlantic Monthly Press, 1999.

Martin, Lesley, ed. Heart of Spain: Robert Capa's Photographs of the Spanish Civil War. New York: Aperture Foundation, Inc., 1998.

Mayer, Henry. All on Fire: William Lloyd Garrison and the Abolition of Slavery. New York: St. Martin's Press, 1998.

McMurry, Linda O. To Keep the Waters Troubled: The Life of Ida B. Wells. New York: Oxford University Press, 1998.

Miller, David. Don't Mention the War: Northern Ireland, Propaganda, and the Media. Boulder, Colo.: Pluto Press, 1994.

Murray, John. The Russian Press from Brezhnev to Yeltsin: Behind the Paper Curtain. Brookfield, Vt.: E. Elgar, 1994.

Nerone, John. Violence Against the Press: Policing the Public Sphere in U.S. History. New York: Oxford University Press, 1994.

Newkirk, Pamela. Within the Veil: Black Journalists, White Media. New York: New York University Press, 2000.

Newton, Eric, ed. Crusaders, Scoundrels, Journalists: The Newseum's Most Intriguing Newspeople. New York: Times Books, 1999.

O'Doherty, Malachi. The Trouble With Guns: Republican Strategy and the Provisional IRA. Belfast, Northern Ireland: Blackstaff Press, 1998.

Ogbondah, Chris W. Military Regimes and the Press in Nigeria, 1966-1993: Human Rights and National Development. Lanham, Md.: University Press of America, 1994.

Rollin, Betty. First, You Cry. New York: Quill, 2000.

Senna, Carl. The Black Press and the Struggle for Civil Rights. New York: F. Watts, 1993.

Simon, Paul. Freedom's Champion: Elijah Lovejoy. Carbondale, Ill.: Southern Illinois University Press, 1994.

Solomon, Martha M. A Voice of Their Own: The Woman Suffrage Press, 1840-1910. Tuscaloosa, Ala.: University of Alabama Press, 1991.

Stille, Alexander, et al. Letizia Battaglia: Passion, Justice, Freedom: Photographs of Sicily. New York: Aperture, 1999.

Stille, Alexander. Excellent Cadavers: The Mafia and the Death of the First Italian Republic. New York: Pantheon Books, 1995.

Stone, Harry. Writing in the Shadow: Resistance Publications in Occupied Europe. Portland, Ore.: F. Cass, 1996.

Streitmatter, Rodger. Unspeakable: The Rise of the Gay and Lesbian Press in America. Boston: Faber and Faber, 1995.

Wells-Barnett, Ida B. Crusade for Justice: The Autobiography of Ida B. Wells. Edited by Alfreda M. Duster. Chicago: University of Chicago Press, 1970.

Wells-Barnett, Ida B. Southern Horrors and Other Writings: The Anti-Lynching Campaign of Ida B. Wells. Edited by Jacqueline Jones Royster. Boston: Bedford Books, 1997.

Whelan, Richard. Robert Capa: A Biography. Lincoln: University of Nebraska Press, 1994.

Whiteman, Kaye, ed. West Africa Over 75 Years: Selections from the Raw Material of History. London: West Africa Pub., 1992.

Youth of the Rural Organizing and Cultural Center. Minds Stayed on Freedom: The Civil Rights Struggle in the Rural South: An Oral History. Boulder, Colo.: Westview Press, 1991.

Index

A

ABC News, 143, 169
Acuña, Rodolfo, 25–26
Adams, John Quincy, 11
Adie, Kate, 132
Africa journalist. *See* West African
  journalist
African Americans. *See* David Ruggles;
  Ida Wells-Barnett; L. Wilson
Afro, 103
Agent, Dan, 128
AIDS. *See* Jeffrey Schmalz
Albuquerque Journal, 124
Alexander, James, 5
American Association of Advertising
  Agencies, 146
American Colonization Society
  slaves back to Africa, 16
  vs Ruggles, 12–13
American Society of Magazine Editors,
  146
Amsterdam News of New York City, 68
Andreotti, Giulio, 82–83
Anti-slavery journalism
  abolitionist and, 11
  California and, 24–25
  Federal gag-rule prohibiting, 11
  Ruggles contributions to, 11–12
  violence against, 11
Arizona Republic, 124, 141
Arkansas State Press, 68
Arviso, Tom Jr., 128
Ashmore, Harry, 103
Aslamazian, Manana, 109

Associated Press, 124
AT&T, 143

B

Babitsky, Andrei, 111
Bagarella, Leoluca, 83
Bailly, Diégou, 162
Ball, John, 59
Baltimore Afro-American, 68
  baseball integration, 101
Baptist Observer, 60
Barnett, Ferdinand L., 33, 35
Barnes and Noble, 147
Barrios, Robert, 117
Bates, Daisy, 68
Bates, L. C., 68
Battaglia, Letizia
  acceptance of, 83–84
  anti-Mafia politicians, 85–86
  characteristics of, 80
  exceptional photographs, 84–85
  impact from pictures, 81
  living location, 80
  Mafia acceptance, 80–81
  murder victim photographing, 79–80
  ordinary photographs, 84
  political career of, 86–87
  political corruption, 81–83
  Sicilian Mafia photographing, 79
Bay of Pigs invasion, 142
Bédié, Henri Konan, 159
  coup d'etat, 165
  vs Quattara, 165
Begay, LeNora, 125

183

Bell, J. Bowyer, 133
Bell, Philip A., 17
Benjamin, Burton, 169
Bennet, Charles, 137
Berezovsky, Boris, 109
Bergman, Lowell, 175–176
Bernstein, Carl, 142
von Bismarck, Otto, 155
Bolles, Don, 141
Boris, Georges, 46
Borovik, Artyom, 110
Borsellino, Paolo, 85
Boudinot, Elias, 122
Boudinot, Tobias, 14
Brandford, William, 4
Breast cancer, mastectomy patient
    interview, 89–97
Breed, Warren, 177
Brenner, Marie, 175
Brent, Joseph Lancaster, 26
British Broadcasting Company (BBC),
    48, 50, 132, 144
Brooklyn Eagle, 21
Broun, Heywood, 102
Brown, Alfred, 55, 64
Brown and Williamson Tobacco Corp.,
    143, 175
Bruce, Walter, 64
Bulgarian National Television, 157
Bunche, Ralph, 72
Buré, Émile, 46
Byelyaninov, Kirill, 109
Byrd, Chief Joe, 128
Byrd, Richard, 57

C

Cahiers de l'O.C.M., 51
California
    cultures combining in, 19–20
    land ownership, 25–26
    liberal ideas in, 23–24
    newspapers of, 21–22
    Ramírez and, 26–28
    settlers of, 21
    slavery and, 24–25
    U.S. expansion, 20
Campbell, Jim, 132
Camus, Albert, 52
Capa, Robert
    bravery reputation, 40–41
    courage of, 41

death of, 43
"Falling Soldier" photograph, 39–40
girlfriend of, 39
growing up, 37–38
Hitler's power and, 38–39
legacy of, 43–44
mentors of, 38
"old school" attitudes, 41–42
photographic focus of, 42
Taro's death, 42–43
Carter, Hodding, 62, 103
CBC, 151–152, 154
CBS, 154
    See also 60 Minutes
Ceux de la Libération, 51
Chabi, Maurice, 162
Chailler, Pierre, 48
Chambers, John, 7
Cherokee Advocate, 128
Cherokee Phoenix, 122
Chesapeake and Ohio Railroad Com-
    pany, 29
Chicago Defender, 35, 68–69, 75
Chicago Inter-Ocean, 34
Chicago Tribune, 142
Child, David Lee, 11, 18
Child, Lydia Maria, 18
Christopher, Warren, 142
Chrysler Corp., 146
Ciancimino, Vito, 82
de la Cierva, Juan, 38
Clarion Ledger, 70
Clarke, Liam, 133
Cockburn, Leslie, 172–173
Colored American, 17
Columbia Journalism Review, 61, 176
Combat, 47, 49, 51–52
Committee to Protect Journalist
    American journalist safety, 171–172
    award program of, 169
    focus of, 170
    independent journalism safety, 171
    journalist insulation, 174–175
    media engines safety, 172–174
    Russia monitoring, 108
Committee of Vigilance
    organization of, 13–14
    Ruggles and, 17
Comonfort, President Ignacio, 26
Conant, Marcus, 116
Conservator, 35

Cornish, Samuel Eli, 12, 17
Corse, Barney, 16
Cosby, Governor William, 3–9
Courage
    award recognizing, 169
    examples of, 141–142
    in journalism, 100
    personal standards as, 170
    small places and, 103–105
    types of, 170
    vs trivialization, 169–170
    See also Journalism

D

D'Agostino, Benedetto, 85
Daily Commercial, 32
Daily Post, 33
Dana, Richard Henry, 21
Darg Case
    city residents attitudes, 15–16
    facts in, 16–17
    Ruggles and, 15, 17
Darg, John P., 16
Davis, Willie B., 60, 64
Davy, Earl, 68, 74
Deal, Percy, 124
Decour, Jacques, 48
Defender, 61
Défense de la France, 47, 49–51
Deiss, Raymond, 47
Deng Ziaoping, 144
Disney World, 143
Dittmer, John, 62
de Dois Unanue, Manuel, 141
Douglass, Frederick, 11, 15, 33
Downing, Kathryn, 148
Dryfoos, Orville, 142
Durant News, 56
Durham, Odell, 61, 64

E

Editor and Publisher, 104, 146, 148
Edmo-Suppah, Lori, 128
Eisner, Isabel, 104
El Clamor Público, 19
    African American advocate, 24
    human rights focus, 23–24
    land ownership disputes, 25
    last issues of, 27–28
    Ramírez and, 22
El Diario/La Prensa, 142

Emancipator, 12–13
Esquire (magazine), 146
Evening Scimitar, 32
Evers, Medgar, 58

F

Faas, Horst, 44
Falcone, Giovanni, 83, 85
Farnham, Thomas Jefferson, 21
Faubus, Governor Orval, 67
Feinstein, Dr. Anthony, 156
Finucane, Dermot, 133
First Amendment
    Cato's letters on, 6–7
    high school students and, 104
    journalism issues, 104
    Zenger trial, 3
Fisher, Mary, 116
Fleming, J. L., 32
Fortune, T. Thomas, 30
France, 46
France Libre, 51
France Soir, 51
France-Amérique, 46
Franco, General Francisco, 38
Frankel, Max, 116
Free Speech and Headlight
    office destruction of, 32–33
    Wells-Barnett and, 29
Freedom Forum, 157
Freedom Neruda
    arrest of, 161–162
    awards of, 162
    media growth and, 160
    as pen name, 159
    vs Bédié, 164–166
Freedom's Journal, 12
French Resistance
    determination of, 49
    free press rebirth, 50–51
    journalist dilemmas, 46
    journalist in, 49–50
    newspaper control, 45–46
    organization of, 47–48
    post-war newspaper growth, 52–53
    post-war newspaper leadership, 51–52
    propaganda of, 47
    repression of, 48–49
    underground publications, 51
    underground press growth, 48

underground publications, 46–47
Friedman, Robert, 170
Friendly, Fred, 102
Fuller, Keith, 74

G

Gallagher, O'Dowd, 39
García, Federico Borrell, 40
Garrison, William Lloyd, 11, 18, 171, 178
Gavin, James, 42
General Electric, 143, 145
Giago, Tim, 104
Gish, Pat, 99
Gish, Tom, 99
Gordon, Thomas, 6
Government, right to criticize, 8–9
Gray, Paul, 24–25
Grossman, Lawrence, 143, 176
Gusev, Pavel, 108
Gusinsky, Vladimir, 109
Gutenberg, Johannes, 4
Guttman, Simon, 38

H

Hamill, Pete, 177
Hamilton, Andrew, 4, 7–8
HarperCollins, 144
Harrison, Francis, 9–10
Hemingway, Ernest, 41
Hersh, Seymour, 142
Hewitt, Don, 176
Hicks, Jimmy, 68
Hispanic Americans. *See* California; Francisco Ramírez
Hoagland, John, 151
Holmes County Herald, 55–56, 58–59
Homosexuality. *See* Jeffrey Schmalz
Hooker, Wilburn, 56, 58
Hopper, Isaac T., 16
Hopper, John, 15
Horthy, Miklós, 38
Hughes, Thomas, 16
Hunter-Gault, Charlayne, 102

I

IBM Corp., 146
Indian Country Today, tribal corruption, 104
Insider (film), story of, 175
International Herald Tribune, 144

Ireland. *See* Northern Ireland

J

Jay, John, 14
Jay, William, 14
Jet (magazine), 60
Johnson, "Magic," 116
Joseph, Elie, 46
Journalism
    "advertorials," 147
    business considerations in, 141
    courage examples, 141–142
    courage in, 100
    early 1900s, 100–101
    editorial integrity, 146
    editorial vs business, 144–145, 147–149
    First Amendment issues, 104
    heroes of, 100
    media size and, 143–144
    national secrets exposing, 142–143
    news presence diminishing, 145–146
    obstacles in, 99–100
    purpose of, 146–147
    risk taking, 143–144
    small place courage, 103–105
    story manipulation, 143
    tribal corruption, 104
    truth vs comfort, 101
    wartime courage, 102

K

Kain, Andrew, 155, 157
Kérékou, Mathieu, 164
Khinstein, Alexander, 112
King, Bill, 102
KMEX-TV, 102
Koop, C. Everett, 147
Koppel, Ted, 169
Korotich, Vitaly, 110
Ku Klux Klan, intimidation by, 71

L

La Crónica, 28
La Estrella de Los Angeles, 22
La Estrella de Occidente, 28
La France Libre, 46
La Lumiere, 46
La Marsillaise, 46
La Voie, 159–160
La Voz del Nuevo Mundo, 28

LaCourse, Richard, 122
Lacy, Sam, 101
Lazareff, Pierre, 46
Le Figaro, 45
Le Franc-Tireur, 47, 49, 51
Le Jour, 162, 165
Le Messager, 163
Le Parisien libéré, 51
Le Petit Parisien, 46
Le Populaire, 46, 51
Le Temoin, 163
Le Temps, 45
L'Echo de Paris, 46
Lee, George, 69
Leichenperg, Harald, 38
Lelyveld, Joseph, 116
Les Echos du Jour, 162
Levy, Leonard, 9
Levy, Louis, 46
Lexington Advertiser, 56
L'Humanité, 51
Libel
    anti-slavery case, 17
    Smith suit, 57
    See also See Zenger trial
Libération, 51
Libération Nord, 47, 51
Libération Sud, 47, 51
Liberty Media, 143
Lima, Salvatore, 82, 85
L'Insurgé, 47
Living Way, 29
L'Œuvre, 46
L'Ora, 79
L'Ordre, 46
Lorillard Corp., 144
Los Angeles Star, 22
Los Angeles Times, 102, 147, 156
Lovejoy, Elijah, 100
Loyd, Anthony, 173–174
L'Université libre, 48
Luzhov, Yuri, 109

M
Maass, Peter, 155
McCarthy, Senator Joseph, 142
McCormick, Robert, 142
McCullen, Don, 131
MacDonald, Peter, 124–127
McDowell, Calvin, 31
McGill, Ralph, 103

McGuinness, Martin, 137–138
McMillen, Neil, 62
McNeer, W. R., 55
Mafia. *See* Letizia Battaglia; Russia
Malashenko, Igor, 110
Mallory, Arenia, 65
Mann, Michel, 175
Maynard, Nancy, 100–101
Medill News Service, 145
Meiselas, Susan, 44
Memphis Daily Appeal, 29
Memphis World, 69
Mesa Tribune, 127
Minkin, Alexander, 112
Minneapolis Tribune, 102
Mirror of Liberty (magazine), 12
Mississippi Free Press, 58, 60
Missouri Press Association, 33
Mitchell, Cathy, 104
Mitchell, Dave, 104
Morin, Relman, 74
Morris, Chief Justice Lewis, 5
Moskovsky Komsomolets, 108, 111–112
Moss, Thomas, 31–32
Mountain Eagle, 99
Mowlam, Dr. Mo, 137
Munka (magazine), 37
Murdoch, Rupert, 144
Murray, Anna, 15
Murrow, Edward R., 142
Musselwhite, George, 55
My Lai massacre, 142

N
Nash, D. D., 14
National Anti-Slavery Standard, 18
Native Americans. *See* Tribal journalism
Navajo Times
    closing of, 127–128
    current status of, 128
    election endorsements, 124–126
    ethics laws and, 125
    financial problems, 126–127
    inauguration coverage, 126
    Tribal election writing, 123–124
    truth seeking and, 128–129
Naynard, Bob, 100–101
NBC News, 142, 145
Ndiaye, Mamadou Oumar, 163
Neal, Claude, 70
Nell, William C., 18

Nelson, C. H., 122
Nerone, John, 171
Neruda, Pablo, 159
New York Age, 30, 32–33
New York Manumission Society, 14, 16
New York Sun, 16, 32
New York Times, 72, 142, 144
New York Times, 102, 154
    gay reporter at, 115–119
New York Times Book Review, 147
New York Times Magazine, 118
New York World, 102
New Yorker (magazine), 146
New-York Weekly Journal, 6–9
News Corp., 144
Newson, Moses, 68, 72, 74
Newsweek (magazine), 145, 151
Nightingale, F., 30
Njawé, Pius N., 163
Northern Ireland
    complexities of, 137–139
    deaths in, 131
    dissent expressing, 134
    freedom of expression in, 134–135
    journalist protocols, 132–133
    news of as respect, 131–132
    nursery slope war of, 131
    peace process vs journalism of, 138–
        139
    society divisions in, 136–137
Northside Reporter, 56
Notre Voie, 164–166
Nourvelliste, 49
Novaya Gazeta, 112
NTV (Russian television), 110–112

O

Oakland Tribune
    advertising ethics, 100–101
    community good instrument, 100
O'Doherty, Malachi
    Northern Ireland, 131–139
    upbringing of, 135–136
Orgill, Edmund, 71
Orlando, Leoluca, 86
Orwell, George, 39
Oswald, Lee Harvey, 102
Ouattara, Alassane D., 164
Owen, John
    Hoagland and, 151–152
    hostile environment training, 154–156

Kosovo conflict, 156–157
risk and career advancement, 153–
    154
Shouf war incident, 152–153

P

Pacino, Al, 176
Paine, Tom, 100
Pantagruel (magazine), 46
Pappas, Ike, 102
Paris-Jour, 51
Paris-Soir, 46
Parks, Michael, 148
Parks, Rosa, 29
Patten, Chris, 144
Payne, Charles M., 62
Penn, I. Garland, 33
Pennington, James W. C., 15
Pennsylvania Gazette, 4, 8
Pentagon Papers, 142
Pétain, Marshal, 45
Phillip Morris Corp., 144
Pitt, Leonard, 22–24
Plummer, Christopher, 177
Point Reyes Light, 104
Politzer, Georges, 48
Popham, Johnny, 72
Pour la victoire, 46
Provisional IRA, 132–133
Public Broadcasting Service (PBS), 142–
    143
Pueblo News, 128
Pulitzer Prize
    Synanon investigation, 104
    winners, 56, 59–61

R

Racism. *See* David Ruggles; Ida Wells-
    Barnett; Hazel Smith; L. Wilson
Ramírez, Francisco P.
    "American" outlook of, 24
    civil liberty beliefs, 19–20
    cultural combining needs, 26–27
    land ownership, 25–26
    Latin American supporters, 26
    liberal views of, 23–24
    Mexican acceptance of, 25
    newspaper editing, 22–23
    political agenda, 27–28
Randall, Henry, 57
Reese, David M., 12

Reid, Betty, 124, 125
Résistance, 47–48
Rice, William B., 22
Ridgway, Matthew, 42
Riina, Salvatore, 82–83
RJR Nabisco Corp., 144
Robinson, Jackie, 101
Roessel, Monty, 124
Rosenthal, A. M., 115
Rowan, Carl T., 102
Ruby, Jack, 102
Ruggles, David
    anti-slavery involvement, 12–13
    Committee of Vigilance and, 13–14
    Darg case and, 15–17
    family history of, 12
    health issues of, 17–18
    newspaper writing of, 17
    newspaper's role, 13
    sea captain's arrests, 14–15
    Underground Railroad and, 15
Russell, John, 17
Russia
    apartment bombing, 110–111
    investigative reporting, 112–113
    journalism politicization, 109–110
    journalist capitulation factors, 108–112
    journalist deaths in, 107–108
    Kremlin censorship criticism, 111
    Mafia wars, 111–112
    media barons serving, 109
    Yudina killing, 107

S
Safer, Morley, 102
St. Louis Globe-Democrat, 62
St. Louis Post-Dispatch, 62
Salazar, Ruben, 102
Salomon, Jacques, 48
Salvo, Nino, 82–83
San Francisco Chronicle, 103
San Francisco Examiner, 104–105
San Francisco Herald, 24
Sangaré, Abou Drahamane, 161
Schmalz, Jeffrey
    acceptance of, 119
    AIDS on-setting, 118–119
    AIDS reporting, 116
    brain seizure of, 115
    as gay, 117–118

sexual orientation hiding, 115
Schmeling, Max, 38
School intergration
    angry crowds against, 67
    black newsmen coverage of, 68–69
    brutality investigations, 69–70
    national guard withdrawals, 67–68
    See also L. Alex Wilson
Seigenthaler, John, 103
Sengstacke, John H., black-owned
    newspapers and, 69
Shaw, David, 148
Shebala, Marley, 128
Shilts, Randy, 103, 116
Sho-Ban News, 121–123, 128
60 Minutes, CBS self-censorship, 177
    courage and, 178
    film portrayal of, 176–177
    Wigand interview non-broadcasting,
        175–176
Smith, Andrew, 59
Smith, Hazel Brannon
    awards of, 62
    black advocate as, 62–63
    black community support, 60–62
    Citizens' Council boycott, 61–62
    civil right evolution of, 58
    as "crusading scalawag," 56
    death of, 63–64
    economic problems of, 60–61
    legacy of, 64–65
    libel suit against, 57
    racist police and, 55–56
    self portrayal, 62
    Supreme Court criticism by, 57
    voter registration campaigns, 59
    vs segregationist, 56–57
Smith, Lemar, 70
Smith, W. Eugene, 44
Smith, William, 5, 7
Soglo, Nicéphore, 163
de Souza, Juan Evangelista, 14
Sovereignty Commission, denouncing of,
    58
Stanford, Leland, 27
State Sovereignty Commission, 56, 58–59
Steward, Henry, 31
Storey, Bobby, 133
Sulzberger, Arthur Jr., 117
Sunday Times, 133

Supreme Court
  California land ownership, 25
  segregated schools opinion, 57

T

Tabouis, Geneviève, 46
Taro, Gerda, 39, 42–43
Tieti, Roch d'Assomption. *See* Freedom
  Neruda
Till, Emmett, 70, 72
Time (magazine), 43, 145
Times, 144, 148
Tisch, Laurence, 144
Todd, Clark, 152
Toolis, Kevin, 133
Trahant, Mark N., 121–129
Treaty of Guadalupe Hidalgo
  military action stopping, 20
  newspaper subsidies from, 22
Trenchard, John, 6
Tri-State Defender, 68, 71–72, 75–76
Tribal journalism
  origins of, 122–123
  potential of, 121–122
  Trahant and, 121–122
  See also Navajo Times
Turnbow, Hartman, 59

U

Ulster Defence Association, 132
Underground Railroad, Ruggles and, 15
Uzcudun, Palino, 38

V

Valmy, 47
Van Dam, Rip, 5
Vanity Fair, 175
Vassilev, Boyko, 157
Vogel, Lucien, 39
Voice of America, 46, 48
Vu (magazine), 39

W

Wall Street Journal, 175
Wallace, Mike, 176
Washington Post, 123, 142, 144
Watergate break-in, 142
Watson, Paul, 156
Weinberger, Casper, 142
Weir, David, 177
Welch, Jack, 145

Wells-Barnett, Ida B.
  court case of, 29
  enemies of, 33
  international attention of, 33
  lynching writing of, 30–33
  lynching statistics publishing, 34–35
  New York Age and, 32–33
  "Princess of the Press," 30
  racial injustice writer, 29–30
  writings of, 33–34
West African journalist
  arrest of, 161–162
  democratic practice respect, 163–164
  French-styled newspapers, 163
  government and, 160
  government criticism by, 163
  independent journalist, 160–161
  journalist courage, 159–160
  legacy of, 163
  political leadership criticism, 164–
    165
  regional recognition of, 162–163
  vs military authorities, 165–166
  See also Freedom Neruda
White, William Allen, 100
Whitman, Walt, 21
Wigand, Jeffrey, 175
Wiley, James T., 57, 60–61
Wiley, Will Edward, 58
Williams, T. M., 58
Wilson, L. Alex
  brutality investigations, 69–70
  death of, 75–76
  education of, 70
  journalism career, 71–72
  newspapers and, 71–72
  physical attack of, 74–75
  racism stories by, 72–73
  racist events effecting, 70–71
  school integration and, 68–69
Withers, Ernest C., 72
Women
  mastectomy patient interview, 89–97
  See also Ida Wells-Barnett; Hazel
    Smith; Letizia Battaglia
Wood, Sue Ann, 62
Woodward, Bob, 142

Y

Yeltsin, Boris, 110
Yudina, Larisa, 107

Z

Zah, Peterson, 124
Zamorano, Augustín, 21
Zecchin, Franco, 79
Zenger, John Peter
  courage of, 9
  profession of, 4
Zenger Trial
  charges in, 3
  controversy beginnings, 4–7

defense attorneys, 7–8
defense strategy, 4
freedom of the press and, 3
jury selection, 7
political control and, 3–4
political power struggle of, 9–10
significance of, 8–9
verdict in, 8
Zenger arrest, 7

For Product Safety Concerns and Information please contact our EU
representative GPSR@taylorandfrancis.com
Taylor & Francis Verlag GmbH, Kaufingerstraße 24, 80331 München, Germany

www.ingramcontent.com/pod-product-compliance
Lightning Source LLC
Chambersburg PA
CBHW050443280326
41932CB00013BA/2217

* 9 7 8 0 7 6 5 8 0 7 9 6 0 *